YOUR recipe could appear in our next cookbook!

Share your tried & true family favorites with us instantly at
www.gooseberrypatch.com
If you'd rather jot 'em down by hand, just mail this form to...
Gooseberry Patch • Cookbooks – Call for Recipes
PO Box 812 • Columbus, OH 43216-0812

If your recipe is selected for a book, you'll receive a FREE copy!

Please share only your original recipes or those that you have made your own over the years.

Recipe Name:

Number of Servings:

Any fond memories about this recipe? Special touches you like to add
or handy shortcuts?

Ingredients (include specific measurements):

Instructions (continue on back if needed):

T0346189

Special Code: **cookbookspage**

Over ➤

Extra space for recipe if needed:

Tell us about yourself...

Your complete contact information is needed so that we can send you your FREE cookbook, if your recipe is published. Phone numbers and email addresses are kept private and will only be used if we have questions about your recipe.

Name:
Address:
City: State: Zip:
Email:
Daytime Phone:

Thank you! Vickie & Jo Ann

I'll Be Home for
Christmas
Cookbook

Holiday favorites for making memories
with those you love

Gooseberry Patch

An imprint of Globe Pequot
246 Goose Lane
Guilford, CT 06437

www.gooseberrypatch.com

1•800•854•6673

Copyright 2020, Gooseberry Patch 978-1-62093-378-7

Do you have a tried & true recipe...

tip, craft or memory that you'd like to see featured in
a **Gooseberry Patch** cookbook? Visit our website at
www.gooseberrypatch.com and follow the
easy steps to submit your favorite family recipe.
Or send them to us at:

Gooseberry Patch
PO Box 812
Columbus, OH 43216-0812

Don't forget to include the number of servings your recipe makes,
plus your name, address, phone number and email address. If we
select your recipe, your name will appear right along with it...
and you'll receive a **FREE** copy of the book!

Contents

Dedication

To everyone who loves freshly fallen snow, children sweetly singing carols and the scent of cookies baking...and knows that all hearts go home at Christmas.

Appreciation

To our family & friends...thank you for sharing your most memorable holiday recipes.

Coming Home
for
Christmas

I'll Be Home for Christmas Cookbook

A Christmas to Remember

Sophia Collins
McHenry, MS

Every Christmas Eve, it has been our family's tradition to have a Christmas Eve party at my mom's home. We would invite those who either didn't have any family nearby, or didn't have family coming that night. One Christmas Eve, my mom was feeling a little down, since my brother Charles had just recently retired from the military. He had been overseas for the last four years and she had yet to see him. He had called a few days earlier and told her he wished he could come home, but he just didn't have the time. On Christmas Eve, we were bustling around trying to get everything set up, since we were anticipating about 40 people. When the tables were full and we were getting ready to pray over the food, I hear a familiar voice calling, "Wait for me!" Lo and behold, when I looked up, here comes my brother and his daughter. They had driven 12 straight hours to make it home in time for the party. I couldn't finish praying because I was crying so hard. What a Christmas to remember! And, all these years later, my mother is still hosting these wonderful gatherings on Christmas Eve.

Coming Home for Christmas

My Earliest Memory Of Christmas

Delores Lakes
Mansfield, OH

I think my earliest memory of Christmas was about 1955, when I was four years old. I remember the song "Silver Bells" playing on the radio in the kitchen as my mother was putting the finishing touches on the family dinner. My grandparents, aunts, uncles and cousins were coming and our white frame farmhouse in Harrisonburg, Pennsylvania would soon be bursting at the seams. I was dancing with excitement as my mother was scurrying around, getting food put in the serving dishes and onto the table as people began to arrive. The thrill of understanding what Christmas was all about made this one extra special. I remember the beautiful doll with jointed arms and legs that I received. She "walked" with me, moving her legs as I held her hand. Her clothing was beautifully detailed with ruffles, two types of fabric and one small pocket. I also received a small chalkboard easel with a box of colored chalk that kept me happily entertained many days after Christmas. There were other years with happy Christmas memories, but this one stands out above all of them!

I'll Be Home for *Christmas* Cookbook

A Sled Ride Home from Brownies

Sharon Demers
Bruce Crossing, MI

I have a fond memory of my father while growing up back east. We lived in New England, where the winters would be full of brisk, cool air and quite the supply of snow. I attended Brownie Scout meetings after school in a quaint, little stone church. Being winter, the days got shorter and the darkness filled the sky. Our Brownie meeting had finished up, where I had just made a special craft. It was a doll ornament made of yarn, a small styrofoam ball, sequins and a roll of Lifesavers candy...the traditional flavors, of course. As soon as I stepped outside, there was my dad with our sled! He had walked all the way from our home to come and get me. I was so excited seeing him there, waiting for me! I can still remember the jacket and gloves he wore while pulling me in the sled. The snow crunched under his feet as we headed for home to mugs of hot cocoa with a dollop of marshmallow creme. I will always remember that sled ride home from Brownies.

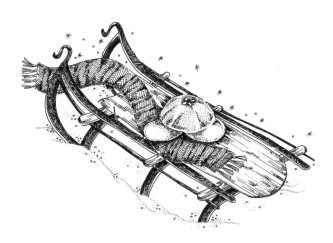

Coming Home
for Christmas

Christmas Cookies for the Firemen

Beverley Williams
San Antonio, TX

Every year I make cookies with my children for Christmas. One day when my oldest was six, a fire truck pulled up to the neighbors' house while we were working on the cookies. It turned out to be a very small fire and everyone was all right. My son asked, "What if there was a fire on Christmas?" and I explained that the firemen worked on Christmas, just in case. He thought it was very sad that they couldn't be with their families on Christmas, but appreciated that they were protecting us. The kids, Nick, John and Hannah (ages six, five and four) decided to make cookies for the firemen and delivered them to the fire house on Christmas morning. This became a family tradition.

Grandpa's Candy Treats

Anita Polizzi
Bakersville, NC

My grandpa loved candy and goodies. We didn't have much money, but at Christmas we knew there would be a cardboard box filled with candy, sitting on my grandma's Singer sewing machine. Everything from chocolate cream drops and orange slices to ribbon candy and pretty coconut balls in pink, green and yellow. There was also stick candy in mixed flavors, horehound candy that was usually saved for winter colds, chocolate-covered peanuts...and my least favorite, chocolate-covered cherries! It seemed like it took forever to decide what to choose. Our Christmas gift was always undies or a slip, Shadowline brand, which was expensive then. I loved my grandparents with all my heart.

9

I'll Be Home for *Christmas* Cookbook

Childhood Christmas

Helen McKay
Edmond, OK

Growing up in Ogden, Utah, Christmas was always fun and exciting. I have so many memories! Searching for the Christmas tree, always coming home with a not-so-perfect one, but Mom making it perfect in our eyes, with icicles, ornaments and lights. Decorating the house, skating on the canal by our house, Dad taking us skiing, my older brother saddling the horse, pulling us behind on our sled and flying around the pasture. Helping Mom make cookies and candy, Dad bringing home a couple of cases of soda, which was a really special treat. Going downtown to walk around the Christmas Village, talking to Santa and giving him our wish list. Family & friends coming and going every day. Family, fun and laughter. I often think of those Christmases some 55 years ago. In my heart, they were the most perfect Christmases, and always will be.

Coming Home for Christmas

Cousins Christmas Party

Monica Britt
Fairdale, WV

Some of my favorite childhood memories include spending Christmas Eve at my grandparents' house with my cousins. It was always such a festive celebration! As time passed, we all grew up and got married, and it became impossible for everyone to get together on Christmas Eve due to scheduling conflicts. After missing our annual Cousins Christmas Eve Party for a few years, we decided to start a new tradition. Now I invited my cousins and their families to my house for a Cousins Christmas Party early in December. Everyone brings a covered dish to share, we reminisce about the good old days, catch up on latest life events, have a few laughs and make new memories together.

I'll Be Home for *Christmas* Cookbook

Fond Memory of Christmas in 1953

Joyce Roebuck
Jacksonville, TX

One of the fondest memories I have is of a Christmas in 1953 when I was a teenager. We lived on a farm and money was scarce. My older sister and I knew not to expect too much for Christmas. I wanted a white leather jacket with fringe, and she wanted a white fleece jacket. We both knew that our parents could not afford them, so we just forgot about it. On Christmas Eve, we opened our gifts, and even though there were no jackets, we were thankful for the gifts we did get. After we had all opened gifts, my father went into another room and came out with two large boxes. Yes, the leather jacket for me and the fleece jacket for my sister! I think that Christmas Eve meant more to me than any other ever has. I think what a struggle it must have been for my parents to be able to buy those jackets. I think of all the gifts that children get nowadays. They couldn't possibly appreciate them as much as we did, for just two jackets and for two unselfish parents.

Coming Home for Christmas

Subs for Christmas

Marcella Smith
Carrollton, OH

One Christmas season, my family was moving into an old farmhouse. Since closing would be the day after Christmas, we spent a freezing cold night in our camper with an inadequate heater. In the morning, we opened our presents on the crowded camper bed. Daddy decided it was too cold to keep us in the camper, so we went back to town to sleep on the floor of our old house. Mom went to get the box of food she had set aside for Christmas dinner, but it couldn't be found anywhere. We ended up at the little convenience store nearby, where they really did not want to make sub sandwiches for eight hungry people on Christmas Day. It was one of the first times I remember seeing tears in Mom's eyes as she explained that without the subs, we would not have any dinner at all. At that point, the workers graciously agreed! Christmas subs are still a wonderful reminder of our adventurous Christmas.

I'll Be Home for *Christmas* Cookbook

The Christmas Tree

Tina Owen
Ghent, KY

My husband and I have had 40 years of Christmases together. We grew up together, I suppose. Before we were married, I would tag along with him to go collect his family's Christmas tree from a farm just up the road from his parents' farm. It seemed there was always snow on the ground back then. It was measured in feet then, not like the inches we get now and again. We'd be bundled up against the cold, but I don't think we ever really felt it. We just felt the joy of being together. It seems like we'd walk forever until we spotted that perfectly shaped cedar tree. The freshness of the glistening snow and the pungent scent of the many evergreens just heightened the Christmas magic. He'd labor, sawing down that perfect tree. Once it was cut, we had the task of trudging it through all that snow, and usually up a hill...slipping and sliding, giggling and laughing. Somehow we'd manage to finally get it to the truck. Of course, by that time it was "flocked" by Mother Nature. Once we got the tree home and stood it up on the porch for his mom to inspect, it was time to place it in that special stand in front of the window. Every year the tree had to be trimmed to fit into the house. No matter how small it looked in the field, it seemed to grow before we got it to the house. It was a thing of beauty with its glistening tinsel and colored lights. The tree wore its adornment of special ornaments with grace and pride, and filled the house with the scent of the outdoors. The years have moved us on and the snows have lessened. The real tree was replaced with an artificial one. Loved ones have passed on, but he and I are still sharing Christmases together and the special memories of all those wondrous Christmases past.

Coming Home for Christmas

My Parents' First Christmas

Elaine Divis
Sioux City, IA

My parents often told the story of their first Christmas, in California in 1942. Mom and Dad were both working to support the war effort. Dad had a bad heart so was classified 4F. As they prepared a chicken for Christmas dinner, they talked about her brother Dick, who was stationed in Palm Springs, preparing to go overseas, and wondering if he would ever come home. Suddenly they heard a knock on the door, and there was Dick! with several of his buddies. They sat down to dinner together, and were always amazed that that small chicken fed so many. And later, Uncle Dick came home safely to Iowa, where they were all from.

Joy, Comfort and Happiness

Arlene Smulski
Lyons, IL

At the Cyrus McCormick Grammar School in Chicago during the 1940s, my classmates had a ten-cent grab bag for Christmas. There were two cardboard boxes wrapped in red and green tissue paper, one for the girls and one for the boys, both decorated with Santas and wreaths. I had met many of my friends at the five & dime store's toy counter, happily picking out cut-outs, jacks sets, tops, toy soldiers, balls and other little gifts. When I came home, wrapping my grab-bag find was such a pleasure. On the day of our humble classroom party, everyone had smiles on their faces...even our dear teacher! We were truly in a joyous holiday mood.

I'll Be Home for *Christmas* Cookbook

A Christmas Wish Come True!

Lou Ann Peterson
Frewsburg, NY

When I was a little girl in the 1960s, I would always go to the local hardware store in our little no-stoplight town with my grandmother. At that time, a lot of older women did not drive, and Grandmother was no exception, so we bundled up and walked to the few stores in our town. The hardware store had a huge toy section and while Grandmother shopped, I would look at all the wonderful toys! Pretty early on that Christmas season (I believe it was 1966) I had fallen in love with the Chrissy doll, whose hair magically "grew." I had asked Santa for that doll and was hoping to get her. On Christmas Eve, some packages appeared under the tree at Grandmother's house...my two brothers and I were so excited! I searched and found a beautiful wrapped box with my name on it. I remember that while the adults finished our traditional Swedish smorgasbord, I just sat there and held on to that package. I was so excited that I almost felt sick to my stomach. Of course, I did get the Chrissy doll and my Christmas was complete. Many, many years later, after my parents and grandparents were no longer living, we were cleaning out the attic at my childhood home. My oldest brother pulled my Chrissy doll out of a box! I can't tell you how excited I was to see her. I'm almost 59 years old now. I still have her now, and I will keep her forever.

Coming Home
for Christmas

Frozen Water Pipes For Christmas

Amy Thomason Hunt
Traphill, NC

It was Christmas Eve of 1989 and my husband and I had just returned home from Okinawa, Japan. The water pipes had frozen in my parents' house and my daddy, brother and brother-in-law decided that they would try to unfreeze them...as we all know, you need running water in the house to cook meals and wash dishes. After hours of working in the cold and snow, the men came in for Christmas Eve dinner. They were half frozen, with ice-cold hands and purple faces. We all enjoyed having everyone sit down to dinner and being together, which unfortunately, ended up being my daddy's last Christmas with us. I can still see him sitting at the dinner table, enjoying his family and our Christmas Eve dinner. It was his favorite time of the year. Christmas is truly a blessing of family and love.

I'll Be Home for
Christmas
Cookbook

The Elf...and Not
the One on the Shelf

Jane Martin
Havre de Grace, MD

When my children were young, we celebrated the twelve days of
Christmas before Christmas, beginning on December 13th, my birthday.
Every night until Christmas Eve, each of our two girls would receive a
small wrapped present placed in a wooden sleigh in their bedroom...
socks, a candy bar, a small toy and sometimes a note from Santa's elf,
encouraging them to be kind to others, do well in school and help out at
home. They couldn't wait to get up every morning to open their gift!
As the girls got older, gift cards replaced the token presents. Now as
adults, they remember the gifts, the gift cards and the encouragement
to "be good" from "The Elf."

'Twas the Night
Before Christmas

Brandi Killian
Coldwater, MI

Every Christmas Eve when I was growing up, I would take part in
my family's Christmas drive-around. We would drive from house to
house, enjoying a little snack or drink at each family member's home,
then ending with a big party at the last house. When we came home,
I would change into my new Christmas pajamas that I'd received, and
prepare a platter of cookies and carrots for Santa and his reindeer. I
never really slept much on Christmas Eve, but I always managed to fall
asleep just long enough to find that platter full of crumbs, and a bursting
Christmas stocking.

Coming Home for Christmas

A Superior Christmas Tree

Lisa Staib
Ash Flat, AR

While living on the fringes of Superior, Colorado, an expensive, ritzy part of town, I would drive through daily to admire the homes, landscaping and decorations. One noontime drive, I noticed a huge eight-foot, pre-lit, artificial Christmas tree left by the curb of a beautiful home. Not wanting to drive off with something from a neighbor, I rang the doorbell to see if this gorgeous tree was in fact free! The owner, who had two huge Great Danes and a three-story marble entryway, said sure, his wife wanted a bigger tree! It must have weighed a hundred pounds! It barely fit in my Suburban and I couldn't figure out what to tell my family. But, here, all these years later, we still have it, and it's beautiful each year.

Christmas at Midnight Mass

Betty Kozlowski
Newnan, GA

Being raised Catholic, we would attend the midnight Mass on Christmas Eve. I remember there was a very large nativity scene set up to the far right of the altar up front. After Mass, we would go up afterwards to check it out. Then we would head home, excited about the gifts that awaited us. There were eight of us kids, so there were lots of presents under our angel hair-adorned tree. Afterwards, pictures were taken of us, in our pajamas with our presents in hand. I don't remember how we ever got to sleep after having to leave our presents!

An Eventful Ice Skating Trip

Deborah Jensen
Tampico, IL

I am very fortunate to have good family memories of life in Clinton, Iowa, where I grew up. One memory in particular, my sister and I will never forget. That winter day, my parents, my sister (age ten) and I (age five) were enjoying various outdoor activities, including building snow forts and snowmen, snowball fights, sledding and ice skating. On that memorable day, we packed the car with extra clothes and blankets, snacks and a thermos of hot cocoa, ice skates and a bushel basket. My dad and my sister were the ice skaters. I fit perfectly in the bushel basket and Dad used the attached clothesline rope to pull me around the pond. My mother was sitting on a log close to the bank, watching all of us on the frozen pond with smiles of joy and love. All of a sudden, we heard several loud cracks and my mother screaming for help. She had fallen through the ice, still sitting on the log in waist-deep frozen water! To this day, my sister and I don't remember how we got our mother out of the water, but we do recall quickly wrapping blankets around her, and Dad driving home as fast as possible. For Christmas this year, I gave my sister a reminder of that eventful day...a room freshener in the shape of a pair of skates with pompoms. We both cherish the memories of that day always.

Coming Home for Christmas

Christmas Eve Hero

Maria Kline
Yucaipa, CA

One year long ago, it was the 24th of December and my family didn't have money for a Christmas tree. I had nine brothers and sisters, and I was the oldest, about 17 years old. I didn't have a car, so I always took the bus. I went to a well-known store, where I saw a Christmas tree on display, already decorated and covered with lights. I bought it super cheap, but I had to carry it like that, cross back and take the bus home. People looked at me and smiled. I barely made it home...it was rainy and the road was muddy. But when I got home with the tree, my siblings were breathtaken and cheering for me. I was a hero for a day! Today I am 72 and they still remember that day. I feel good remembering, too!

I'll Be Home for
Christmas
Cookbook

Waiting to Unwrap the Gifts

Narita Roady
Pryor, OK

To me as a child, Christmas was amazing and waiting to open gifts was torment. We opened our presents on Christmas Eve night. After a wonderful meal, I was ready to run to the tree and get started...I had been looking at my gifts for a month! Suddenly Mother became a sloth doing the dishes. When she was finally done, she meticulously set out a scrumptious tray of homemade goodies...banana bread, pumpkin bread, date nut loaf, fudge, haystacks and divinity candy. Now! Nope, she had to make coffee for her and Dad! Finally we were around the tree! To prolong my suffering, she had a rule of opening one gift at a time, taking adequate time to oohh and ahhh over what the person had gotten, putting the wrappings in a trash bag and only then going on to the next gift. Ugh! As a child I hated this, but as an adult, I see our tradition through different eyes and am thankful for it. Mother was savoring the moment, not only of the holiday but of our family too. Now I am thankful and look back on the time with humor and warm feelings.

Coming Home for Christmas

A Visit from Santa

Deanna Harrison
Flagstaff, AZ

My memory starts when I was very young. On Christmas Eve, my sister, my little cousin and I always went to bed early at my grandparents' house to wait for Santa to come. Once we kids had fallen asleep, the adults, including our aunts and uncles, would put all the presents under the tree. Then a short time after midnight, my grandpa and two of my uncles would climb up on the roof, stomp around and Grandpa would yell, "Ho-Ho-Ho!" We kids would jump out of bed and race into the living room, where the tree was full of presents. We would run outside, where my aunt would spot a plane in the air (of course, we didn't know it was a plane!) and say, "Look, it's Rudolph!" We would wave at Santa and the reindeer, go inside and tear open the presents. I know as a kid, the presents were what mattered, but as an adult, it is my favorite holiday memory that my family would go to so much trouble, just to make sure we kids knew that Santa had come. This happened every year, even when I was old enough to know the truth..and I still loved it!

I'll Be Home for *Christmas* Cookbook

Christmas Morning Memories

Cheryl Flynn
Mount Sterling, IL

I am one of six kids, and on Christmas morning we sat on the steps in order from youngest to the oldest, waiting to go in the living room to see what Santa had brought. Santa left our presents unwrapped, under the Christmas tree in six piles, one for each kid. It was always so exciting to see all those presents under the tree. My oldest sister, who lives out of state, and I have had Santa "deliver" our kids' presents to our parents' house every Christmas, and still continue to do so even though our kids are grown. Now our parents are gone, but our youngest sister still lives in their house, so our Christmas traditions live on. My sister's kids are 27 and 29, and my son is 20, but we still make them sit on the steps in order of their age, and "Santa's" presents are still unwrapped under the tree in a pile for each one. Our Christmas memories are wonderful and hopefully our kids will carry on our tradition.

Festive Holiday
Brunch

Pineapple Upside-Down French Toast

Janis Parr
Ontario, Canada

*This breakfast dish is delicious and a huge hit with everyone.
It's especially nice to serve to overnight guests.*

8 thick slices egg bread,
    crusts removed
6 eggs, beaten
1-1/2 c. milk
1/4 c. sugar
1 t. vanilla extract
1/4 t. cinnamon

2 T. butter, melted
3/4 c. brown sugar, packed
20-oz. can pineapple slices,
    drained
Garnish: maple syrup or other
    favorite topping

Arrange bread slices in a large shallow dish; set aside. In a large bowl, beat together eggs, milk, sugar, vanilla and cinnamon. Pour egg mixture over bread slices. Turn bread slices over; allow them to soak up remaining milk mixture for at least 10 minutes. May also cover and refrigerate overnight. Spread melted butter in the bottom of a 13"x9" baking pan. Sprinkle brown sugar evenly over butter, pressing it into the butter. Arrange pineapple slices over brown sugar; top each slice with a slice of soaked bread. Bake, uncovered, at 375 degrees for 30 to 40 minutes, until bread is puffy and golden. Serve piping hot, garnished as desired. Makes 4 to 8 servings.

Simple touches say "welcome" when family & friends come to visit...a snowman doormat, Christmas dishes and music playing cheerily in the background will get everyone in the holiday spirit.

Festive Holiday *Brunch*

White Hot Chocolate

Debbie Manning
Grandview, IA

*I love white chocolate...it's even better in a mug
of hot chocolate!*

3 c. half-and-half, divided
2/3 c. white chocolate chips or
   melting chocolate, chopped
3-inch cinnamon stick

1/8 t. nutmeg
1 t. vanilla extract
1/4 t. almond extract
Optional: cinnamon to taste

In a large saucepan, combine 1/4 cup half-and-half, chocolate, cinnamon stick and nutmeg. Whisk over low heat until chocolate is melted. Remove cinnamon stick; add remaining half-and-half. Cook, whisking often, until heated through. Remove from heat; stir in extracts. Serve in warm mugs, sprinkled with cinnamon, if desired. Makes 5 servings.

Just for fun, set out snowman-shaped candy
marshmallows for folks to float in their hot cocoa!

Spinach & Bacon Skillet Quiche

*JoAnn
Gooseberry Patch*

This hearty breakfast dish will fortify you for shoveling snow or chopping down the perfect Christmas tree...or simply celebrating the holidays! I like to use a cast-iron skillet, then set the skillet on the buffet table for serving. It keeps the quiche nice and warm.

12 slices bacon	1/2 t. nutmeg
1 T. oil	1/2 t. onion powder
3 c. frozen shredded	1/4 t. salt
hashbrowns, partially thawed	1/2 t. pepper
5 eggs, beaten	1 c. fresh baby spinach
1-1/2 c. milk	1 c. shredded Cheddar cheese

In a large skillet over medium heat, cook bacon until crisp. Set bacon aside to drain on paper towels. Drain drippings from skillet; add oil and heat over medium heat. Spread hashbrowns in the bottom and up the sides of pan. Cook for 5 minutes, or until potatoes form a crust. In a large bowl, whisk together eggs, milk and seasonings. Sprinkle spinach and crumbled bacon evenly over potatoes; pour egg mixture over top. Cover and cook over medium-low heat for 10 minutes. Sprinkle with cheese. Cover and cook another 5 minutes, or until eggs are set and cheese is melted. Cut into wedges. Makes 6 servings.

If your extended family finds it a challenge to get together on Christmas Day, why not enjoy a brunch together one weekend? Relax with each other over coffee and fruit juice, baskets of warm muffins and a yummy breakfast casserole. You'll be glad you did!

Festive Holiday *Brunch*

Vanilla-Glazed Cranberry Bread

Kimberly Ascroft
Rockledge, FL

We love cranberries, but aren't fond of the usual cranberry dressing. So this recipe came about! This delicious loaf is always welcome at the breakfast table. Fresh blueberries or blackberries can also be used instead of cranberries.

1-1/2 c. all-purpose flour
2 t. baking powder
1/2 t. salt
1-1/2 c. fresh cranberries,
   rinsed and patted dry
1 c. plus 2 T. sugar, divided

1 c. vanilla yogurt
1/2 c. oil
3 eggs, beaten
1/2 t. vanilla extract
1 T. lemon juice

In a bowl, combine flour, baking powder and salt; mix well and set aside. In a large bowl, mash cranberries with one cup sugar; stir in yogurt, oil, eggs and vanilla. Add flour mixture to cranberry mixture; stir until well combined. Pour batter into a lightly greased and floured 9"x5" loaf pan. Bake at 350 degrees for 45 minutes; remove from oven. Meanwhile, in a small bowl, combine lemon juice and remaining sugar; stir until a sugary paste forms. Poke holes in the top of the hot bread with a fork; brush sugary paste over bread. Return to oven for 5 minutes, or until sugar is glazed and crystallized. Makes one loaf.

Use a holiday tea towel to wrap up a loaf of fresh-baked quick bread. The wrapping will be a lasting gift too!

I'll Be Home for *Christmas* Cookbook

Christmas Brunch Casserole

Lyneen Burrow
Cicero, IN

I have been making this recipe for well over 25 years. Our grown kids still ask for it on Christmas morning! It's delicious, easy and I always have the ingredients on hand.

1 lb. ground pork breakfast
   sausage
8-oz. tube refrigerated crescent
   rolls
8-oz. pkg. shredded mozzarella
   cheese

4 eggs, beaten
3/4 c. milk
1/4 t. salt
1/8 t. pepper

Brown sausage in a large skillet over medium heat; drain well. Line the bottom of an ungreased 13"x9" baking pan with crescent rolls, pressing perforations together. Sprinkle with browned sausage and cheese. Combine eggs, milk and seasonings in a bowl; whisk together well and pour over sausage. Bake, uncovered, at 425 degrees for 15 minutes, or until set and golden. Let stand 5 minutes before serving. Cut into squares. Makes 6 servings.

Slip jingle bells onto colorful pipe cleaners, then twist into cheery napkin rings...a holly jolly jingle to wake everyone at breakfast!

Festive Holiday Brunch

Sticky Pecan Buns

Vickie
Gooseberry Patch

Oooey-gooey goodness...guaranteed smiles at the breakfast table! Put them together the night before, then in the morning you just pop them in the oven and serve.

3/4 c. chopped pecans
24 frozen dinner rolls
3-1/2 oz. pkg. cook & serve
   butterscotch pudding mix

1/2 c. butter
3/4 c. brown sugar, packed
1 t. cinnamon

Sprinkle pecans in a greased 13"x9" baking pan; arrange rolls over pecans. Sprinkle dry pudding mix over rolls; set aside. Melt butter in a small saucepan over low heat. Add brown sugar and cinnamon; cook and stir until brown sugar melts. Pour mixture over rolls. Loosely cover pan with plastic wrap sprayed with non-stick vegetable spray. Set pan in a warm place. Let rolls rise for 8 hours or overnight. Bake at 350 degrees for 25 to 30 minutes. Turn out rolls onto a large tray; serve warm. Makes 2 dozen.

Hot Spiced Tea

Laura Parker
Claremont, NC

I remember my mother making this tea for our Christmas visitors when I was a little girl. Not only does it give everyone that warm fuzzy feeling, but the aroma when you walk through the door is a special scent of Christmas!

5 c. water, divided
5 to 6 tea bags
1 c. sugar
30 whole cloves

1 c. orange juice
1 c. pineapple juice
1/2 c. lemon juice

In a saucepan over high heat, bring 4 cups water to a boil; remove from heat. Add tea bags and let steep. In a large saucepan over medium-high heat, bring remaining water, sugar and cloves to a full boil for 3 to 5 minutes. Remove cloves. Add juices; discard tea bags and add hot tea. Heat through over low heat; serve warm. Makes 8 cups.

Freezer Sausage Balls

Connie Ramsey
Pontotoc, MS

This recipe produces very tender sausage balls. They are great for breakfast or appetizers! I am always asked for the recipe, and when I carry these little treats to any event, there are never any left! They freeze beautifully, and I often give bags of these frozen treats to friends at Christmastime. Having a batch of them in the freezer comes in very handy when people drop by during the holidays!

1 lb. ground pork sausage
8-oz. pkg. shredded sharp
   Cheddar cheese

2 c. biscuit baking mix
1/4 c. water

Brown sausage in a large skillet over medium heat. Drain well and let cool. Combine sausage and cheese in a food processor; gently pulse several times. Transfer sausage mixture to a large bowl. Add baking mix and water; stir gently until mixed. Shape into one-inch balls; place on a baking sheet coated with non-stick vegetable spray. Cover with aluminum foil and freeze. When completely frozen, remove balls to a plastic zipping bag; return to freezer. When ready to bake, place desired number of sausage balls on a sprayed baking sheet. Bake at 400 degrees for 15 to 20 minutes, or until golden. Serves 12.

Welcome everyone home with the scent of Christmas.
In a saucepan, combine a quartered apple, slices of orange
peel and whole spices like cinnamon sticks, rosemary
sprigs, cloves and ginger. Cover with water
and set to simmer over low heat...sweet!

Festive Holiday *Brunch*

Delicious Brunch Potatoes

Cyndy Rogers
Upton, MA

Breakfast or brunch isn't complete without a pan of these delectable golden potatoes. So delicious, yet so easy!

8-oz. pkg. shredded mild
    Cheddar cheese
16-oz. container sour cream
10-3/4 oz. can cream of
    chicken soup
1 T. onion, chopped

1/2 c. butter, divided
32-oz. pkg. frozen diced
    hashbrown potatoes, partially
    thawed
3 c. corn flake cereal, crushed

In a large bowl, combine cheese, sour cream, soup, onion and 1/4 cup melted butter. Mix well; add potatoes and stir until well mixed. Spoon into a greased 13"x9" baking pan. Mix corn flakes and remaining melted butter; sprinkle on top. Bake, uncovered, at 350 degrees for 45 to 60 minutes, until bubbly and golden. Serves 10.

A sweet favor for any children coming to your holiday brunch! Fill a basket with little bags of "Reindeer Food" for kids to sprinkle on the lawn on Christmas Eve. To make, simply mix cereal rings with candy sprinkles.

I'll Be Home for *Christmas* Cookbook

Mini Apricot Scones with Honey Butter

Margaret Welder
Madrid, IA

My husband is fond of dried apricots. Our daughter found this recipe years ago and it has become one of his favorites. We all love scones, perhaps because I'm part English. I have shared this recipe with many others. The honey butter is a recipe from a friend of mine. It is so yummy that you could eat it with a spoon!

2 c. all-purpose flour
1/3 c. sugar
1 T. baking powder
1/2 t. salt
1/4 t. nutmeg
1 t. orange zest

1/2 c. cold butter
3/4 c. half-and-half
1 egg, beaten
1/2 c. dried apricots, diced
Optional: additional sugar

In a large bowl, combine flour, sugar, baking powder, salt, nutmeg and orange zest. Cut in cold butter with a fork until mixture is crumbly. In another bowl, whisk together half-and-half and egg. Add to flour mixture along with apricots; stir until just combined. Turn out dough onto a floured surface; knead 10 times. Pat or roll out to 3/4-inch thickness. Cut into 2-inch rounds with a biscuit cutter. Place on a parchment paper-lined baking sheet. (May also pat dough into a 9-inch circle. Cut into 8 wedges; do not separate before baking.) Sprinkle with sugar, if desired. Bake at 400 degrees for 10 minutes, or until golden. Serve with Honey Butter. Makes 6 to 8 scones.

Honey Butter:

1/2 c. whipping cream
1/2 c. honey

1/2 c. sugar
1 c. butter, softened

In a saucepan over low heat, combine whipping cream, honey and sugar. Cook and stir until sugar dissolves; remove from heat. In a bowl, beat butter with an electric mixer on medium speed until creamy. Gradually add hot cream mixture; continue beating for 4 to 5 minutes, until fluffy. Transfer to a container; cover and chill until firm. May keep refrigerated for several weeks. Makes about 2-1/2 cups.

Festive Holiday *Brunch*

Honey-Glazed Ham Biscuit Sliders

Carol Hickman
Kingsport, TN

These little sandwiches are a new favorite at our house. We served these at a New Year's Eve celebration and they were a huge hit with everyone. We only had one slider left on the platter at the end of the evening. I think it was left simply because no one wanted to be seen taking the last one! This recipe is easily doubled to serve a larger group.

12 buttermilk biscuits,
    baked and split
3 to 4 slices baked spiral ham
3 to 4 slices Baby Swiss or
    provolone cheese

1/4 c. butter, melted
1/3 c. honey

Arrange bottom halves of biscuits on an ungreased baking sheet; set aside. Cut ham and cheese into biscuit-size pieces. Top biscuit bottoms with a slice of ham, a slice of cheese and tops of biscuits. In a small bowl, whisk together melted butter and honey. Spread butter mixture lightly over tops of biscuits. Bake, uncovered, at 400 degrees for 8 minutes, or just until biscuits are golden and cheese has melted. Remove from oven. Let cool in pan for a few minutes before removing, so glaze can set up. Serve warm. Makes 12 sliders.

Peace on earth will come to stay
When we live Christmas every day.
–Helen Steiner Rice

Gingerbread Biscuits

Kitty Thomason Brown
Traphill, NC

I make these for my family every Christmas. We think they are exceptionally good...I hope you'll try them!

5 c. all-purpose flour, divided	1/2 c. margarine, softened
1 t. baking soda	1/2 c. sugar
1/2 t. salt	1 egg, beaten
1 t. cinnamon	3/4 c. molasses
1 t. ground ginger	1 c. buttermilk
1/4 t. ground cloves	

In a bowl, sift together 2-1/4 cups flour, baking soda, salt and spices; set aside. In a separate large bowl, blend margarine, sugar and egg. Add flour mixture and mix well; stir in molasses and buttermilk. Stir in enough of remaining flour to make a stiff dough. Cover and refrigerate for 8 hours or overnight. On a floured surface, roll out dough to 1/8-inch thick; cut out with a biscuit cutter. Place on lightly greased baking sheets. Bake at 350 degrees for 8 to 12 minutes. Makes 2 dozen.

"A taste of home" is a thoughtful gift for a friend who has moved away. Pack up some locally made goodies like jam or cheese. Tuck in picture postcards, holiday newspaper clippings and a photo of your family holding a sign that says, "Merry Christmas from back home!" She'll love it.

Festive Holiday Brunch

Vanilla Citrus Fruit Salad

JoAnn
Gooseberry Patch

We all love this fresh fruit salad for Christmas breakfast.

2 navel oranges, peeled and
    sectioned
1 grapefruit, peeled and
    sectioned
2 c. fresh pineapple cubes

2 T. lime juice
1/4 c. powdered sugar
1/2 t. vanilla extract
Garnish: vanilla Greek yogurt,
    citrus zest

Cut citrus fruits into bite-size pieces and place in a large bowl. Add pineapple cubes; set aside. In a small bowl, whisk together lime juice, powdered sugar and vanilla. Drizzle over fruit and toss to combine well. Cover and refrigerate for 20 minutes before serving. Garnish servings with a dollop of yogurt and a sprinkle of zest. Makes 4 to 6 servings.

Holiday Wassail

Zolane Gordon
Mercer, PA

Over the years, this has become a holiday tradition to serve with our Christmas brunch. It's a favorite at office holiday gatherings too.

2 qts. apple cider
4 c. orange-pineapple juice
1/2 c. lemon juice
1/2 c. sugar

12 whole cloves
4 4-inch cinnamon sticks
Optional: orange slices,
    additional cloves

In a Dutch oven, combine all except optional ingredients. Bring to a boil over high heat. Reduce heat to medium-low; simmer for 10 to 15 minutes. Remove whole spices; serve warm. If desired, stud orange slices with cloves; float in a heat-safe punch bowl. Makes about 3-1/2 quarts.

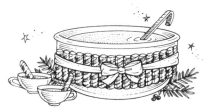

Scrambled Egg, Ham & Cheese Casserole

Leah Beyer
Columbus, IN

My family enjoys this every morning after family holidays. The men request it and the kids can't get enough! It's easy to make ahead the night before, then pop in the oven to serve.

2 c. cooked ham, diced
7 T. butter, melted and divided
1 doz. eggs, beaten
4-oz. can sliced mushrooms, drained
2-1/4 c. soft bread crumbs

Prepare Cheese Sauce; set aside. Meanwhile, in a large skillet over medium heat, sauté ham in 3 tablespoons butter. Add eggs; cook, stirring occasionally, just until eggs are set. Fold in mushrooms and Cheese Sauce. Spoon egg mixture into a greased 13"x9" baking pan. Toss together bread crumbs and remaining butter; spread evenly over egg mixture. Cover and chill overnight. Uncover; bake at 350 degrees for 30 minutes, or until heated through. Makes 10 to 12 servings.

Cheese Sauce:

2 T. butter
2-1/2 T. all-purpose flour
2 c. milk
1/2 t. salt
1/8 t. pepper
1 c. pasteurized process cheese, diced

Melt butter in a saucepan over medium heat; blend in flour and cook for one minute. Gradually stir in milk; cook until thickened. Add salt, pepper and cheese; stir until cheese melts. Set aside.

A fringed red plaid throw makes a festive runner for a brunch table.

Festive Holiday *Brunch*

Hot Cocoa in a Slow Cooker

Teri Austin
Jenks, OK

I served this at a "Christmas Chocolate Party" for my Lunch Bunch group from church. Each person brought a potluck chocolate yummy to share...it was so much fun! The hot cocoa was easy to keep ready in the slow cooker and super chocolatey yummy!

1-1/2 c. whipping cream
14-oz. can sweetened
   condensed milk
2 c. milk chocolate chips

4 sqs. sweet baking chocolate,
   chopped
6 c. whole milk
1 t. vanilla extract

Combine all ingredients in a 3 to 4-quart slow cooker. Cover and cook on low setting for 2-1/2 to 3 hours, stirring occasionally, until hot, chocolate is completely melted and well blended. Makes 12 to 15 servings.

Carolyn's Candied Bacon

Georgia Muth
Penn Valley, CA

This recipe was given to me by my cousin. This yummy bacon can be served as an appetizer or with breakfast...it's always a hit!

1/2 lb. thick-sliced bacon
1/2 c. finely chopped pecans
1/2 c. brown sugar, packed

1/4 t. cayenne pepper
3 T. pure maple syrup

Line a 15"x10" jelly-roll pan with aluminum foil; set a wire rack in pan. Arrange bacon slices on rack; bake at 400 degrees for 10 to 12 minutes. Meanwhile, in a small bowl, combine pecans, brown sugar and cayenne pepper; stir in maple syrup. Remove bacon from oven; spoon pecan mixture onto bacon slices. Bake another 5 minutes. Remove from oven and spread melted mixture over bacon; bake another 5 minutes. Cut slices in half for serving. Serves 6.

Set out peppermint sticks for stirring cocoa...
after all, it's Christmas!

Cherry Coffee Cake

Lori Simmons
Princeville, IL

Any kind of pie filling can be used in this easy coffee cake. Cherry is especially pretty for Christmas...apricot is very good too!

4 c. biscuit baking mix
1/2 c. sugar
3 eggs, beaten
1/2 c. plus 1-1/2 T. milk, divided
1/4 c. butter, melted
1 t. vanilla extract
21-oz. can of cherry pie filling
1 c. powdered sugar

In a large bowl, combine baking mix, sugar, eggs, 1/2 cup milk, butter and vanilla; stir well. Spread half of batter in a greased 15"x10" jelly-roll pan. Spread pie filling over batter. Drop spoonfuls of remaining batter over pie filling. Bake at 350 degrees for 20 to 25 minutes. Stir together powdered sugar and remaining milk to a drizzling consistency; drizzle over coffee cake. Cut into squares. Serves 15.

Monkey Bread with a Twist

Wendi Knowles
Pittsfield, ME

One Christmas when my children were quite young, I made this recipe for our breakfast...I think they liked this more than the gifts under the tree! Now they are all grown up, and I still make it every Christmas. They tell me the smell of the bread baking brings back wonderful memories. My grandson loves it too.

2 loaves frozen bread dough, thawed
2 11-oz. pkgs. milk chocolate drops, unwrapped
1/2 c. butter, melted
1/4 c. cinnamon
1 c. sugar

Tear bread dough into silver dollar-size pieces; wrap each around a chocolate drop. Place melted butter in a bowl; combine cinnamon and sugar in a separate bowl. Dip dough balls into butter; roll in cinnamon-sugar. Layer balls in a greased fluted cake pan, filling pan 3/4 full; do not fill pan as it will overflow. Bake at 350 degrees for 45 minutes, or until lightly golden. Best served warm. Serves 12.

Festive Holiday *Brunch*

Ice Cream Cinnamon Rolls

Janel Hull
Wellsville, KS

When I was a child, my mother always made cinnamon rolls for Christmas morning. While Dad, my sisters and I were enjoying the excitement of Christmas morning and seeing what Santa brought us, Mom was in the kitchen, making the cinnamon rolls for us to enjoy. I wanted to continue this tradition with my own family, but I also wanted to be able to enjoy the kids' enthusiasm on Christmas morning. This recipe was shared with me years ago. It's now one of my family's favorites, and of course a Christmas morning tradition!

1 c. pecan halves
12 frozen thaw & rise cinnamon
   rolls with frosting packet
1/2 c. sugar

1/2 c. brown sugar, packed
1/2 c. vanilla ice cream
5 T. butter

The night before, spread pecans in a greased 13"x9" stoneware dish or baking pan. Return frosting packet to refrigerator; arrange frozen rolls over pecans. (May do half pecans, half without, for those who don't care for nuts.) In a saucepan over medium-high heat, combine sugars, ice cream and butter; bring to a boil for one minute. Pour over cinnamon rolls. Set in the cold oven overnight. The next morning, turn on the oven; bake at 350 degrees for 20 to 30 minutes, until golden. (No need to preheat oven.) Drizzle with reserved frosting, as desired. Makes one dozen.

Ho-Ho-Ho! Invite a local Santa to drop in during a family get-together. What a joy for all ages!

Good & Ready Oat Bran Muffins

Janis Parr
Ontario, Canada

With this recipe, you can mix up your muffin batter, then keep it in the fridge until you're ready to bake the number of muffins you want. So convenient...tasty too! I've made these many times when asked for baked goods for the food booth at the fair.

2 c. natural wheat bran	4 eggs
2 c. boiling water	2 t. vanilla extract
5 c. all-purpose flour	1 qt. buttermilk
5 t. baking soda	4 c. rolled oats, uncooked
1 t. salt	1-1/2 c. golden raisins or
1 c. shortening	chopped dates
3 c. sugar	

Place bran in a bowl. Pour boiling water over bran; set aside. In a large bowl, stir together flour, baking soda and salt; set aside. In another bowl, blend shortening and sugar. Add eggs, vanilla and buttermilk; stir to combine. Add shortening mixture to flour mixture and stir well. Add bran mixture, oats and raisins or dates; stir just until combined. Spoon batter into greased muffin cups, filling 3/4 full. Bake at 375 degrees for 15 to 20 minutes, until muffins test done with a toothpick. Keep unused batter refrigerated until ready to use, up to 2 months. To bake, use batter directly from refrigerator; bake at 375 degrees for 20 to 25 minutes. Makes 5 dozen.

Tuck a packet of fresh-baked muffins into a pretty gift basket of breakfast foods like spiced tea, jams & jellies. So thoughtful for welcoming a new neighbor!

Festive Holiday *Brunch*

Holiday Cranberry Honey Butter

Jill Ball
Highland, UT

This is a holiday favorite! I make a huge batch to keep on hand during the holidays. It's delicious on toast, muffins, pancakes...just about anything. It makes a great gift with a homemade loaf of bread.

1 c. butter, softened	1/4 c. honey
1/3 c. finely chopped dried cranberries	2 t. orange zest
	1/8 t. salt

In a small bowl, beat all ingredients until blended. Cover and refrigerate up to 2 weeks. Makes 24 servings, or about 1-1/2 cups.

Christmas Jam

Donna Smith
Wilmington, DE

Christmas jam for Christmas breakfast! Easy and delicious... the little jars make great gifts too.

12-oz. pkg. fresh cranberries	4 c. sugar
2 10-oz. pkgs. frozen strawberries, thawed and juice reserved	3-oz. pkg. liquid pectin
	12 1/2-pint canning jars with lids, sterilized

Coarsely chop cranberries in a food processor. Combine cranberries, strawberries with juice and sugar in a Dutch oven. Being to a boil over medium heat; cook for one minute. Remove from heat; stir in pectin. Return to a full boil for one minute; skim off any foam. Ladle jam into hot sterilized jars, leaving 1/4-inch headspace. Wipe rims; add lids. Process in a boiling-water bath for 5 minutes; set jars on a towel to cool. Check for seals. Makes one dozen 1/2-pint jars.

I'll Be Home for *Christmas* Cookbook

Green Chile Sausage Swirls

Kim Neely
Georgetown, TX

We've enjoyed this recipe over the years. My mother-in-law started the tradition of having our "swirls" on Christmas morning before opening gifts. Once we started having Christmas morning at home, I began to make them for my own family's tradition. Since they're prepared ahead of time, you only need to bake them...so easy! Now we also add mimosas to the Christmas morning. My family loves it all!

4 c. biscuit baking mix
1/2 c. butter, melted
1 c. milk
1 lb. ground hot pork sausage

1 lb. ground mild pork sausage
1-1/2 c. canned or fresh chopped
    green chiles

Place baking mix in a large bowl; cut butter into biscuit mix. Stir in milk. Cover and refrigerate for 30 minutes. Meanwhile, in a separate bowl, combine uncooked sausages and chiles; let stand to room temperature. Divide dough in half. On a lightly floured surface, roll out each half into a large rectangle, 1/4-inch thick. Spread half of sausage mixture completely over each half of dough. Roll up jelly-roll style, starting on one long edge. Wrap in plastic wrap; freeze for only one hour. Remove from freezer; slice 1/3-inch thick. Place slices on a baking sheet, with wax paper between layers of slices; freeze. When ready to bake, place frozen slices on a baking sheet. Bake at 400 degrees for 20 to 25 minutes. Makes 4 to 5 dozen.

Keep it simple on Christmas morning. Instead of preparing a fruit salad, set out a bowl brimming with bright-colored clementines. Kids especially like these juicy little peel & eat oranges!

Festive Holiday Brunch

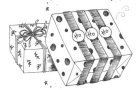

Mini Ham & Cheese Frittatas
Joyceann Dreibelbis
Wooster, OH

This is a quick & easy appetizer to make for a Christmas Eve get-together or a Christmas brunch. To spice it up, add a tablespoon of chopped fresh chives or green onions to the egg mixture before spooning into the muffin cups. These reheat well in the microwave.

2 whole eggs
3 egg whites
1 T. water
1/2 t. dill weed

1/4 c. shaved deli honey ham, finely chopped
3/4 c. extra sharp shredded Cheddar cheese

In a bowl, whisk together whole eggs, egg whites and water until blended. Stir in dill weed and ham. Spoon into mini muffin cups coated well with non-stick vegetable spray; top with cheese. Cheese will sink slightly. Bake at 350 degrees for 18 to 20 minutes, until puffed and golden. Serve warm. Makes 8 to 10 pieces.

Decorate the kitchen for the holidays! Tie cheery bows on cabinet knobs, hang cookie cutters in the window and tuck sprigs of fresh pine into sifters, mixing bowls and canisters.

Mixed Fruit Salad

Carolyn Gochenaur
Howe, IN

I have made this fruit salad many times. It is so good served with brunch...a very colorful dish. Canned and drained mandarin oranges and pineapple chunks can be used instead of the fresh. Basically, use your favorite fruits!

1 apple, cored and cubed
1 navel orange, peeled and
   sections cut in half
1 pear, cored and cubed
1 c. fresh pineapple cubes
3 kiwi, peeled and sliced
2 c. red or green seedless grapes

1 pt. fresh strawberries, hulled
   and halved
21-oz. can peach pie filling
6-oz. jar maraschino cherries,
   drained and rinsed
1 pt. fresh blueberries
2 to 3 ripe bananas, sliced

Combine all ingredients in a large glass bowl, adding blueberries and bananas last. Stir just to coat every piece of fruit and serve immediately. Refrigerate any leftovers. Serves 10 to 12.

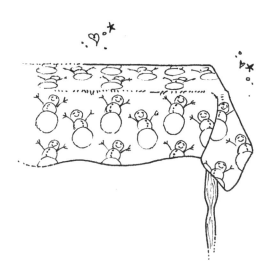

An oilcloth tablecloth with brightly colored reindeer or snowmen is cheerful at breakfast...sticky syrup and jam spills are easily wiped off with a damp sponge.

Festive Holiday Brunch

Crustless Broccoli, Cheese & Sausage Quiche

Sheila Craig Peregrin
Lancaster, PA

I adapted this recipe when I was on a low-carb diet. Now it is our favorite breakfast casserole! It also makes a nice appetizer, baked in a square glass pan and cut into bite-sized squares. Serve with a side of fruit for breakfast, or a salad with a tangy dressing for brunch. Versatile and yummy!

6 turkey breakfast sausage links, thinly sliced
10-oz. pkg. frozen chopped broccoli
1 c. shredded 2% Cheddar cheese
1 c. cottage cheese
1 T. dried, chopped onion
1 T. frozen diced red and green peppers
1 t. dried or canned fire-roasted tomatoes, diced
seasoned salt to taste
3 eggs

Combine all ingredients except eggs in a large bowl; set aside. Beat eggs in glass measuring cup; whisk in enough water to equal 3/4 cup. Add egg mixture to large bowl; stir well. Pour into a greased 10" glass pie plate. Bake at 350 degrees for about 45 minutes, watching closely the last 10 minutes, until set and lightly golden around the edges. Let stand several minutes; cut into wedges. Makes 6 servings.

A coffee mug rack makes a clever holder for displaying several favorite Christmas ornaments...perfect for a party table or buffet.

Ham & Swiss Quiche

Gwen Hudson
Madison Heights, VA

Years ago, my children would not eat the original Quiche Lorraine, calling it hot egg pie. A friend gave me this recipe and my family loved it! Smoked deli ham is good in this.

9-inch deep-dish pie crust, unbaked
1-1/2 c. cooked ham, diced
1-1/2 c. Swiss cheese, cubed
1/3 c. green pepper, finely chopped
1/3 c. onion, finely chopped
1/2 c. mayonnaise
1/2 c. milk
2 eggs, well beaten
1 T. cornstarch

Bake pie crust at 400 degrees for about 10 minutes. Meanwhile, combine remaining ingredients in a large bowl. Mix well and pour into pie crust. Bake at 400 degrees for 10 minutes. Reduce heat to 350 degrees; bake for another 45 to 50 minutes, until a knife tip inserted in the center comes out clean. Cut into wedges to serve. Makes 6 to 8 servings.

Turn refrigerated cinnamon rolls into snowmen. Arrange rolls in a snowman shape on a baking sheet and bake as directed. Top with fluffy white icing and add faces with raisins or mini candies. Festive and fun!

Festive Holiday Brunch

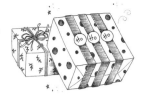

Cheesy Hashbrown Bites

Nancy Wise
Little Rock, AR

These little morsels are great for a brunch or appetizer buffet

6 slices bacon
1 egg, beaten
1/2 c. sour cream
salt and pepper to taste

1-1/2 c. shredded sharp
  Cheddar cheese
20-oz. pkg. frozen shredded
  hashbrowns, thawed

Cook bacon in a skillet over medium heat until crisp; drain. Crumble and set aside. Meanwhile, in a large bowl, whisk together egg, sour cream and seasonings. Fold in cheese, hashbrowns and bacon. Scoop into balls by heaping tablespoonfuls; place in greased mini muffin cups. Bake at 425 degrees for 20 minutes, or until golden. Makes about 2 dozen.

Warm-Me-Up Hot Chocolate

Mel Chencharick
Julian, PA

*I love mocha coffee on a cold winter's day! If you do too,
this is quick & easy.*

4 c. boiling water
1/3 c. instant cocoa mix
1/4 c. instant coffee granules

Garnish: whipped topping or
  marshmallow creme

Bring water to a boil in a saucepan over high heat. Stir in cocoa mix and coffee granules. Ladle into mugs; garnish as desired. Makes 4 to 6 servings.

'Tis Christmas morning:
Christmas mirth, and joyous
voices fill the house.

–Thomas Bailey Aldrich

Cranberry Oatmeal Delight

Gladys Kielar
Whitehouse, OH

This is a delicious warm dessert for cold weather...
a perfect end to a holiday brunch!

1-1/2 c. apples, peeled,
   cored, cubed
15-oz. can whole-berry
   cranberry sauce
1 c. rolled oats, uncooked

1/2 c. brown sugar, packed
1/4 c. all-purpose flour
1/4 c. butter, melted
1/2 t. salt
1/2 c. chopped pecans

In a saucepan over medium heat, cover apples with water. Cook until apples are tender. Drain and transfer to a bowl; mix in cranberry sauce. Spoon into a buttered 10"x6" baking pan. In another bowl, combine oats, sugar, flour, butter and salt; spread over cranberry mixture. Sprinkle pecans over top. Bake, uncovered, at 350 degrees for 50 minutes, or until hot and bubbly. Cool slightly. Makes 10 servings.

Gingerbread Granola

Sybil Pritchard
Knoxville, TN

Try this granola sprinkled over yogurt with fresh fruit, or as a cold cereal all by itself! This would also make a great gift packed in a Mason jar, with a bit of fabric and ribbon tied around the lid.

4 c. rolled oats, uncooked
1 c. chopped walnuts or pecans
1/2 c. molasses
2 T. canola oil

1 t. cinnamon
1 t. ground ginger
1 c. raisins

In a large bowl, mix together all ingredients except raisins. Spread evenly on a parchment paper-lined 15"x10" jelly-roll pan. Bake at 325 degrees for 30 to 35 minutes, stirring after 15 minutes. Let cool on the pan; stir in raisins. Store in a covered container. Serves 10.

Christmas
Open House

Christmas Cheese Ball

Cherilyn Dunn
Fairborn, OH

This is a favorite at our holiday parties. It just isn't Christmas without this pretty red and green cheese ball on the table! It looks great on a platter with crackers and sliced fruit.

2 8-oz. pkgs. cream cheese, softened
1 c. grated Parmesan cheese
2-oz. jar chopped pimentos, drained
4 t. green pepper, chopped
1/2 t. garlic salt
1/2 c. chopped walnuts
snack crackers

Combine cheeses in a large bowl; stir until blended. Add pimentos, green pepper and garlic salt; mix well. Form into 2 balls or one large ball. Roll in chopped walnuts; wrap in plastic wrap. Refrigerate until set. Serve with your favorite crackers. Serves 12.

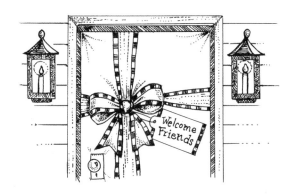

Invite friends & neighbors to an afternoon holiday get-together. Serve lots of easy-to-make appetizers, punch and sparkling cider. Keeping it casual and fuss-free means you have lots of time to catch up on each other's holiday plans.

Christmas
Open House

Grandma's Chicken Delight

Elizabeth Smithson
Mayfield, KY

This is an old favorite that's been in my family for years. I always serve it at Christmas parties. For cocktail parties, make larger balls and roll in chopped parsley. Both ways are good!

1/2 c. cream cheese, softened
2 T. mayonnaise-style salad
    dressing
1 c. cooked chicken, finely
    chopped
1 c. slivered almonds

1 T. fruit chutney
1 to 1-1/2 t. curry powder,
    to taste
1/2 t. salt
1/2 c. flaked coconut

In a large bowl, blend cream cheese and salad dressing. Add remaining ingredients except coconut; mix well. Shape into marble-size balls and roll in coconut. Chill in a covered bowl until serving time. Makes 3 dozen.

Serve easy-to-handle foods and beverages at tables in several different stations around the house. There will be plenty of room for guests to snack and mingle easily.

Nutty Cheddar Cheese Log

Ursula Juarez-Wall
Dumfries, VA

I first made this way back in my 7th grade home economics class. It was so delicious that I kept the recipe and made it several years later at a family holiday dinner. It disappeared very quickly and I knew the recipe was a keeper! Great with crackers and fruit.

8-oz. pkg. shredded sharp
    Cheddar cheese
3-oz. pkg. cream cheese,
    softened
2 T. milk
1 T. Dijon mustard

1 t. Worcestershire sauce
1/2 t. hot pepper sauce
1 T. butter
1/3 c. chopped pecans
1/4 t. seasoned salt
2 t. dried parsley

In a large bowl, combine cheeses, milk, mustard and sauces. Beat with an electric mixer on medium speed until well blended. Cover and chill until firm, about one hour. Meanwhile, melt butter in a small skillet over low heat until bubbly. Sauté pecans until crisp and lightly golden, about 5 minutes, stirring often; cool slightly. Chop pecans finely and return to skillet. Stir in seasoned salt and parsley; set aside. On wax paper, with a spatula or moistened hands, shape chilled cheese mixture into a 7-inch log. Roll in pecan mixture until well coated. Wrap tightly in plastic wrap; chill until firm. Serves 10 to 12.

Christmas is the season of joy, of gift-giving,
and of families united.

–Norman Vincent Peale

Christmas Open House

Holiday Guacamole

Marla Kinnersley
Surprise, AZ

My friend of 30 years, Jen, shared a simpler version of this recipe with me. I have played around with the recipe until it became this amazing holiday guacamole, which gets eaten up every single time it's put out. Everyone wants to know what's in it, because it's so darn good! If you can find red and green tortilla chips, arrange them around the bowl to look like a festive wreath. Enjoy!

3 ripe avocados, peeled, pitted
   and diced
1-1/2 c. seedless red grapes,
   quartered
1 c. pomegranate seeds
1 jalapeño pepper, seeded
   and minced

3 T. fresh cilantro, chopped
3 T. red onion, diced
2 cloves garlic, minced
juice of 1 lime
1/2 t. salt
1/8 t. pepper
tortilla chips

In a large bowl, mash avocado with a fork to desired texture. Add remaining ingredients except tortilla chips; mix well. Transfer to a festive serving bowl; serve with your favorite tortilla chips around it. Makes 8 servings.

When decorating the Christmas tree, keep extra-special ornaments at eye level and above. Then, place unbreakable ornaments on lower branches...an ideal solution for curious little ones and pets!

Mini Dogs in Sauce

Janice Tarter
Morrow, OH

Our family has served this at parties for many years. It wouldn't be a party without these wienies! This is so much better than just buying a jar of barbecue sauce and pouring it over them. It takes a little more time, but the results are worth it. Yummy!

20-oz. bottle catsup
1 c. brown sugar, packed
1/3 c. bourbon or apple juice
6 T. lemon juice
3 T. vinegar
2 T. Worcestershire sauce
2 T. dried, minced onion
2 t. minced garlic
several drops smoke-flavored
  cooking sauce
1 t. dry mustard
2 t. salt
1/2 t. pepper
3 12-oz. pkgs. hot dogs, cut into
  bite-size pieces

Combine all ingredients except hot dogs in a 3-quart slow cooker. Mix well; add hot dogs and stir until well coated. Cover and cook on low setting for 3 to 4 hours, until hot and bubbly. Serve with toothpicks. Serves 20.

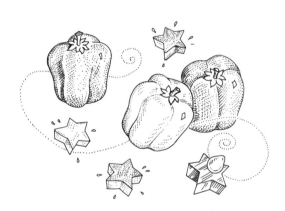

Cut out bite-size pieces of fresh red and yellow pepper with
a star-shaped mini cookie cutter...what a clever way
to trim a veggie dip platter!

Christmas
Open House

Slow-Cooked Cranberry Meatballs

Ann Tober
Biscoe, AR

This is my go-to easy party food! The cranberries make it perfect for serving at Christmas parties.

12-oz. can jellied cranberry sauce
12-oz. jar chili sauce
10-oz. jar red pepper jelly
2 T. brown sugar, packed
several shakes hot pepper sauce
32-oz. pkg. frozen meatballs

Combine all ingredients except meatballs in a 3-quart slow cooker. Add meatballs and stir to coat well. Cover and cook on low setting for 6 to 8 hours, or on high setting for 2-1/2 hours. Serves 12 to 15.

Bacon-Wrapped Water Chestnuts

Cindy McKinnon
El Dorado, AR

I was at a friend's birthday party and someone had brought this delicious appetizer. Being a water chestnut lover, I couldn't eat just one! I asked for the recipe, fixed it for my family the next day and they loved it too. These are really good warmed up again too.

2 8-oz. cans water chestnuts, drained
1 lb. bacon, each slice cut into 3 pieces
1/2 c. brown sugar, packed
1/2 c. catsup

Wrap each water chestnut in a piece of bacon; fasten with a wooden toothpick. Arrange on a baking sheet coated with non-stick cooking spray. Bake at 400 degrees for 45 minutes to one hour, or until bacon is crisp. Combine brown sugar and catsup in a bowl; spoon over chestnuts. Reduce oven to 350 degrees; bake for an additional 30 to 45 minutes, until glazed. Serves 12.

Dress up an appetizer tray with frilly toothpicks for serving.

Smoked Salmon Paté

*Ronda Morhaime
Rogersville, TN*

Every year I order smoked salmon from Washington State, where my son lives. He makes sure I receive my shipment before Thanksgiving and I share it all through the holidays. I use a small copper fish mold for this, but any gelatin mold or bowl will work.

8-oz. pkg. cream cheese,
  softened
1/4 to 1/3 lb. smoked salmon,
  flaked
1 T. onion, finely minced
1 t. lemon juice

1 clove garlic, pressed
1/2 t. prepared horseradish,
  or to taste
1-1/2 t. fresh parsley, minced
toasted baguette slices or
  pita wedges

In a large bowl, combine cream cheese, salmon, onion, lemon juice, garlic, horseradish and parsley. Mix well. Line a gelatin mold or bowl with plastic wrap; press salmon mixture into mold. Cover and refrigerate at least 2 hours or overnight, to allow flavors to blend. Unmold onto a serving plate. Surround with toasted baguette slices or pita wedges. Serves 12.

Make a party tray of savory bite-size appetizer tarts... guests will never suspect how easy it is! Bake frozen mini phyllo shells according to package directions. Cool, then spoon in a favorite creamy dip or spread.

Christmas
Open House

Sassy Shrimp Spread

Sena Horn
Payson, UT

Whenever there is a party, I'm asked to bring this dip. Simple and yummy, it tastes delicious with crackers or fresh veggies. It's sassy, with a little kick! It's easy to double for a larger crowd...and it's rare to have any leftovers!

8-oz. pkg. cream cheese, softened
1/2 c. mayonnaise
4-oz. can tiny cocktail shrimp, drained and rinsed
1/2 c. onion, finely chopped
2 T. seafood cocktail sauce
1/8 t. garlic salt
1/8 t. lemon pepper

Combine cream cheese and mayonnaise in a bowl; stir until well blended. Add remaining ingredients; blend well. Cover and refrigerate until serving time. For the best flavor, serve at room temperature. Serves 8 to 10.

Bev's Sparkling Fruity Party Punch

Lisa Ann Panzino DiNunzio
Vineland, NJ

My mom serves this punch every year at our annual Christmas open house, and at other events throughout the year. It goes super quickly, it's that good! And, it's ready to serve in a jiffy.

2 1-qt. bottles cranberry-grape juice, chilled
2 2-ltr. bottles lemon-lime soda, chilled
1 gal. rainbow sherbet

Pour one bottle of fruit juice and one bottle of soda into a large punch bowl; stir gently. Add 5 to 7 scoops of sherbet to the bowl and serve. Add more juice and soda as punch is served; add more sherbet as desired once it melts into the punch. Serves 25 to 30.

A tasty tip...make an ice ring of fruit juice
to keep punch from becoming diluted.

Candied Dream Mix

Jane Luke
Valrico, FL

The bowl is emptied quickly whenever these treats are around! My husband adores this mix so much and we give packages of it as holiday gifts. You can substitute your favorite chips for the white chocolate chips. At Easter, I use pastel candies and bunny-shaped crackers, and at Halloween, orange and brown candies.

3 c. bite-size crispy chocolate rice cereal squares
5 c. bite-size crispy corn & rice cereal squares
4 c. fish-shaped cheese crackers
2 c. fish-shaped pretzels
1-1/2 c. pecan halves
1 c. cashews or peanuts
1/2 c. macadamia nuts or almonds
2 c. butter
2 c. brown sugar, packed
2 c. candy-coated chocolates
3/4 c. white chocolate chips

In a very large bowl, combine cereals, crackers, pretzels and nuts; mix well and set aside. In a heavy saucepan over medium heat, combine butter and brown sugar. Bring to a boil, stirring constantly; boil and stir until frothy. Pour hot butter mixture over cereal mixture, stirring as you pour. Toss to coat. Spread mixture evenly on 2 lightly greased 15"x10" jelly-roll pans. Bake at 250 degrees for 10 minutes; stir. Continue baking for another 45 minutes, stirring several times. Remove from oven; cool completely. Add chocolate candies and chips; toss well. Cool and store in an airtight container, or package for gifting. Serves 36.

A glass storage jar is perfect for gifts of tasty snack mix. Just fill, add a bright-colored pom-pom in the lid and it's ready for giving.

Christmas
Open House

Top-of-the-Christmas-List Snack

Taryn Rice Williams
Raleigh, NC

Throughout the year and especially at Christmas, I get requests from family & friends for this tasty snack. I store and reuse an extra-large disposable turkey roasting pan for ease of mixing the ingredients. Just mix and enjoy...no cooking or baking required!

12-oz. pkg. crispy hexagon-
    shaped corn & rice cereal
6-oz. pkg. small flat pretzels
9-oz. pkg. corn chips

8-1/2 oz. pkg. crunchy
    cheese puffs
1 c. cashews
1 c. pecan halves

In a large container, combine cereal and pretzels; stir in corn chips and cheese puffs. Add nuts and stir. It's helpful to add the nuts last because they tend to sink to the bottom. The snack mix keeps well stored in either airtight containers or plastic zipping bags. Makes about 16 cups.

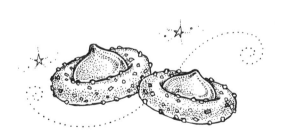

For the sweetest bite-size treats, arrange round or waffle pretzels on a baking sheet; place a chocolate drop in the center of each. Bake at 350 degrees for one to 2 minutes; remove from oven and press a chocolate-coated candy into the centers. Chill before serving. Yummy!

I'll Be Home for *Christmas* Cookbook

GrandMary's Seafood Plate

Nancy Albers Shore
Cheyenne, WY

This is a popular appetizer in our family, especially at the holidays. It's one of the recipes I found in my husband's grandmother's recipe box, and I am pleased to share it with you. Grandma Mary decided that she needed a name with fewer syllables, so she became GrandMary to us, and her memory lives on in our hearts and her recipes! "Light" products may be used for this, but for the best flavor, don't use fat-free products.

8-oz. pkg. cream cheese, softened
1 c. sour cream
1/4 c. mayonnaise
1 c. seafood cocktail sauce, or to taste
1 c. cooked shrimp, chopped, or 4-oz. can medium shrimp, drained

6-oz. can crabmeat, drained and flaked
1 c. green pepper, chopped
1/2 c. green onions, sliced
1 c. shredded mozzarella or Monterey Jack cheese
snack crackers and/or tortilla chips

In a large bowl, blend cream cheese, sour cream and mayonnaise until combined. Spread evenly onto a serving platter; top evenly with cocktail sauce. Layer shrimp, crabmeat, pepper and onions over sauce. Cover and chill until ready to serve. Just before serving, sprinkle with shredded cheese. Serve with crackers and/or tortilla chips. Serves 6 to 8.

Start a notebook of your favorite tried & true holiday recipes. Each Christmas, add notes about what worked well and what you'd do differently. Remember to label family members' favorites...even add photos of family get-togethers. What a sweet tradition!

Christmas
Open House

Warm Spinach-Artichoke Dip

Carol Lytle
Columbus, OH

Everyone's favorite hot dip! Serve with white tortilla chips or your favorite snack crackers.

8-oz. pkg. cream cheese, softened
1/3 c. mayonnaise
2 cloves garlic, finely chopped
1/2 t. Italian seasoning
9-oz. pkg. frozen chopped spinach, thawed and very well drained

6-oz. jar marinated artichoke hearts, well drained and chopped
1 c. shredded mozzarella cheese
1/4 c. shredded Parmesan cheese

Combine cream cheese, mayonnaise, garlic and seasoning in a bowl; mix well. Fold in remaining ingredients. Transfer to a lightly greased one-quart casserole dish. Bake, uncovered, at 350 degrees for 25 minutes, or until heated through. Let stand 10 minutes before serving. Makes 8 to 10 servings.

Serve a favorite dip or spread with toasty homemade baguette chips. Thinly slice a loaf of French bread. Arrange slices on a baking sheet and spray lightly with non-stick olive oil spray. Bake at 350 degrees for 10 minutes, or until crunchy and golden.

I'll Be Home for *Christmas* Cookbook

Matt's Jalapeño Popper Dip

Wendy Reaume
Ontario, Canada

My husband Matt loves jalapeño poppers and asks for them anytime the game is on. They take some effort to put together, so I decided to try my popper recipe as a dip. It became an immediate favorite! This dip has been a regular request at parties ever since.

8 large jalapeño peppers, halved
    and stems trimmed
1 to 2 T. olive oil
2 8-oz. pkgs. light cream cheese,
    softened
1 c. light mayonnaise

1-1/2 c. shredded Cheddar
    cheese
1 c. panko bread crumbs
1/2 c. grated Parmesan cheese
1/4 c. margarine, melted
tortilla chips

Remove and discard veins and seeds from jalapeños. In a large bowl, toss jalapeño halves with oil; place on a broiler pan. Broil under a 500-degree broiler for 5 minutes per side, or until edges start to char. Remove from oven; turn oven to bake setting at 400 degrees. Finely chop jalapeños to form a paste. In same bowl, mix together jalapeños, cream cheese, mayonnaise and Cheddar cheese until well combined. Spread in a lightly greased one-quart casserole dish. In a separate bowl, mix together panko crumbs, Parmesan cheese and margarine until soft crumbs form. Sprinkle evenly over top. Bake, uncovered, at 400 degrees for 20 to 25 minutes, or until bubbly and golden. Serve with tortilla chips. Serves 8.

Be sure to protect your hands with plastic gloves when preparing fresh jalapeño peppers. A serrated grapefruit spoon makes short work of removing the seeds.

Christmas
Open House

Taco Fried Chicken Wings

Josh Logan
Victoria, TX

These spicy wings will jazz up your next appetizer buffet...
or treat the kids to them for dinner one night!

2 eggs
2 T. water
1/3 c. all-purpose flour
1-oz. pkg. taco seasoning mix
1/2 t. salt

2 lbs. chicken wings, separated
3/4 to 1 c. canola oil
Garnish: ranch salad dressing or
   taco sauce

In a shallow dish, whisk together eggs and water. In another dish, mix flour, taco seasoning and salt. Dip wings into egg mixture; shake off excess egg and coat in flour mixture. In a large skillet, heat 3/4 cup oil over medium-high heat to 350 degrees. Working in batches, add several wings to skillet. Cover and cook for 4 minutes per side, until golden and juices run clear when pierced. If wings cook too quickly, reduce heat to medium; add more oil as needed. Drain on a wire rack placed over paper towels; repeat with remaining wings. Makes 12 to 16 wings.

Best-Ever Slush Punch

Leona Krivda
Belle Vernon, PA

This is something I like to serve at Thanksgiving and at Christmas.
Who doesn't like a good punch, right?

46-oz. can pineapple juice
46-oz. can orange juice
1 c. sugar
1 c. water

4 c. red fruit punch
2 qts. ginger ale, chilled
Optional: orange slices

Add all ingredients except ginger ale and orange slices to a clean 5-quart plastic pail. Mix well; cover and freeze. Remove from freezer 4 to 5 hours ahead to thaw a little. Chop up with a knife to make a slush. Transfer to a punch bowl; add ginger ale just before serving. If desired, float orange slices on top. Makes 50 small servings.

I'll Be Home for *Christmas* Cookbook

Spicy Mini Sausage Sandwiches
Amy Mattock
Fairfax, VA

My mom was an excellent cook and a gracious hostess, and she loved the Christmas season. Every Christmas Eve, she and my dad hosted a family dinner for my birthday, which falls on Christmas. This appetizer was always on the dinner menu and reappeared at Christmas breakfast the following morning. Though Mom is no longer with us, we try to carry on her tradition and our Christmas menu is incomplete without these little sausage sandwiches.

1 lb. ground hot pork sausage
1 lb. ground beef
1 lb. pasteurized process
   cheese, cubed

1 t. Worcestershire sauce
garlic salt to taste
16-oz. loaf cocktail rye bread

Brown sausage and beef together in a large skillet over medium heat, stirring to crumble. Drain; add cheese and cook until melted, stirring occasionally. Add Worcestershire sauce and garlic salt to taste. Arrange bread slices on baking sheets. Place a spoonful of sausage mixture on each slice of bread. Freeze on baking sheets for several hours or overnight. Transfer frozen slices to plastic freezer bags; return to freezer. To serve, place slices on baking sheets; bake at 350 degrees for 15 to 20 minutes. Makes 15 servings.

Santa's Lil' Sausages
Jill Ball
Highland, UT

One of my family's favorite traditions is sitting around the Christmas tree on Christmas Eve, eating appetizers. We talk, laugh and eat...such a good time!

2 14-oz. pkgs. mini smoked
   sausages
3/4 c. cola

18-oz. bottle sweet barbecue
   sauce

Add sausages to a 3-quart slow cooker; set aside. In a bowl, combine cola and barbecue sauce. Stir well and pour over sausages. Cover and cook on high setting for 1-1/2 hours, or on low setting for 2-1/2 hours. Serve with toothpicks. Serves 14.

Christmas Open House

Mulled Cranberry Wassail

Rosemary Trezza
Tarpon Springs, FL

My family shares this version of wassail every Christmas Eve before dinner. As we all pitch in on the finishing touches for dinner, we enjoy a cup of this wassail. It gives us a warm and cozy feeling...perfect for a special evening.

1/2 gal. apple cider or juice
4 c. cranberry-raspberry juice
   cocktail

2 T. brown sugar, packed
3 4-inch cinnamon sticks
5 orange slices

Combine juices in a large saucepan over medium-high heat; bring to a boil. Reduce heat to medium; stir in remaining ingredients. Keep beverage hot over low heat; serve in mugs. Serves 8 to 10.

Christmas Tortilla Roll-Ups

Melissa Flasck
Rochester Hills, MI

This recipe was created for my son's first daycare Christmas party. I wanted to serve something red and green and came up with this fun finger food!

8-oz. pkg. cream cheese,
   softened
1/2 c. mayonnaise
0.6-oz. pkg. zesty Italian salad
   dressing mix

1 t. dried parsley
1/2 c. red pepper, diced
1/2 c. green onions, chopped
5 8-inch flour tortillas

In a bowl, blend cream cheese, mayonnaise, dressing mix and parsley until smooth. Add pepper and onions; blend well. Spread mixture evenly over tortillas; roll up. Wrap rolls individually in plastic wrap; refrigerate for at least one hour. At serving time, cut each roll into one-inch slices. Serves 8.

Sriracha Caramel Corn

Jessica Kraus
Delaware, OH

This spicy treat has become a fan favorite when handing out Christmas tins to our family & friends. Sweet and salty caramel corn with a little bit of heat on the back end. Add some mixed nuts, if you like.

6 c. popped popcorn
1/2 c. butter
3/4 c. brown sugar, packed
1/4 c. light corn syrup

1/8 t. salt
1-1/2 t. sriracha hot chili sauce
1/2 t. vanilla extract
1/4 t. baking soda

Place popcorn in a large bowl; remove any unpopped kernels and set aside. Melt butter in a saucepan over medium heat. Stir in brown sugar, corn syrup and salt. Bring to a boil; let the mixture boil for 4 minutes. Remove from heat; stir in remaining ingredients. Pour mixture over popcorn; stir until evenly coated. Spread popcorn evenly on parchment paper-lined baking sheets. Bake at 250 degrees for 45 minutes, stirring well every 15 minutes. Remove from oven; let cool. Store in an airtight container. Makes 7 cups.

Encourage everyone to sing favorite Christmas carols...
don't worry if you're off key, you'll be sensational!

Christmas
Open House

Yummy Spiced Toffee Nuts
Ashley Compoli
Ontario, Canada

*This is a great recipe to make around Christmastime.
It won't stay around for long, though!*

1 egg white
2/3 c. sugar
1/2 c. honey
1 t. ground ginger

1 t. nutmeg
1 t. cinnamon
4-1/2 c. mixed nuts

Beat egg white in a bowl until frothy. Add remaining ingredients except nuts and mix well. Fold in nuts, coating well. Spread nut mixture on a greased rimmed baking sheet. Bake at 350 degrees for 20 minutes, stirring often. Spread nuts in a single layer to cool, making sure they are quite separated so they don't get stuck together. Break into bite-sized pieces; store in a covered container. Serves 8 to 10.

Pick up some extra disposable icing cones when you shop for baking supplies. Filled with small treats, tied with ribbon and placed in a wire cupcake stand, they make sweet gifts to keep on hand for Christmas visitors.

I'll Be Home for
Christmas
Cookbook

Game-Side Hot Chocolate

Sue Nance
Sand Springs, OK

Ever since I found this recipe, we have enjoyed it at football games, parades and around the campfire. I especially enjoy it with a good book on a cold evening! The grandkids love theirs topped with marshmallows and I enjoy a dollop of whipped cream.

25-oz. pkg. non-fat dry milk
16-oz. jar powdered non-dairy
  creamer
16-oz. container chocolate drink
  mix

13-oz. jar malted milk powder
1 c. sweet chocolate & cocoa
  beverage mix
1 c. powdered sugar

Combine all ingredients in a very large container. Use a wire whisk to be sure it is well mixed and distributed evenly. (May process in a food processor to make it a fine powder.) Store in a plastic zipping bag or divide into jars with tight lids; attach directions. Directions for one serving: add 2 to 3 tablespoons of mix to a mug. Fill mug with boiling water (or hot milk for even richer cocoa) and stir well. May add more or less mix to taste. Makes a very large amount.

A vintage canning jar filled with homemade cocoa mix makes a wonderful gift. Tie on a topper of colorful holiday fabric with ribbon, along with directions for enjoying your gift.

Christmas
Open House

Frank's Soda Cracker Snack

Beverly Elkins
Bloomington, IN

This recipe was given to me by Frank, my neighbor of 40 years, as he was moving from our hometown to Florida at the age of 84. He loved making this snack and sharing it with friends and neighbors. He asked that each time I make his snack, I think of him and our longtime friendship. I do! A great sweet & salty treat.

1 sleeve saltine crackers   1 c. light brown sugar, packed
1 c. butter

Line a baking sheet with aluminum foil; spray with non-stick vegetable spray. Arrange crackers on baking sheet in a single layer; set aside. In a saucepan over medium heat, melt butter with brown sugar. Cook until foamy, about 3 minutes. Let cool slightly; spoon over crackers. Bake at 350 degrees for 10 minutes. Let cool; refrigerate on baking sheet until chilled. Remove snacks to a plastic zipping bag. Serves 8 to 10.

Pecan Crackers

Jane Moss
Cranberry, PA

These crackers are very addictive and are a great party-pleaser. People can't eat just one! This is a great Christmas gift for people like my nephews who are hard to buy for.

1-1/2 sleeves club crackers   2/3 c. sugar
1/2 c. butter   1 c. chopped pecans

Line a 15"x10" jelly-roll pan with aluminum foil; spray with non-stick vegetable spray. Arrange crackers on baking sheet in a single layer, breaking some crackers to fit around the edges; set aside. Melt butter in a saucepan over medium heat; stir in sugar. Bring to a boil; boil for 3 minutes. Spoon over crackers and spread around. Sprinkle pecans over crackers. Bake at 300 degrees for 20 to 25 minutes. Remove from oven; when cool enough to handle, break apart. For best flavor, let stand several hours before serving. Serves 20.

I'll Be Home for
Christmas
Cookbook

Colorful Fresh Salsa

Marian Forck
Chamois, MO

This salsa is sweet yet has a little kick to it...it's delicious with chips and crackers. My friend Debbie gave me this recipe while we were getting together to play cards. I added a few other ingredients of my own. Great for get-togethers of all kinds!

1 mango, peeled, pitted and diced
1 avocado, peeled, pitted
    and diced
4 tomatoes, diced
11-oz. can sweet corn &
    diced peppers
1/2 c. fresh cilantro, chopped
1/4 c. red onion, diced

3 T. garlic, minced
1 jalapeño pepper, seeded and
    minced, or 2 T. canned diced
    green chiles
3 T. olive oil
2 T. lime juice
1 T. red pepper flakes
1 t. salt

In a bowl, combine mango, avocado, tomatoes, corn, cilantro, onion, garlic and jalapeño; stir well. Stir in remaining ingredients. Cover and chill for 30 minutes before serving. Serves 12 to 16.

Live music makes any gathering extra special for guests!
Ask a nearby school to recommend a music student
who would enjoy playing Christmas carols on piano,
violin or guitar.

Christmas
Open House

Dilly Dilly Shrimp Dip

Rosemary Lightbown
Wakefield, RI

I started making this simple dip almost 40 years ago for our Christmas Eve celebration. It has become our oldest daughter Sarah's all-time favorite. I still make it every year...and often in between!

8-oz. pkg. cream cheese,
    softened
1/4 c. milk
1 c. small shrimp, or 4-oz. can
    small shrimp, drained
1 t. Worcestershire sauce

1 t. lemon juice
1/2 t. dill weed
1/2 t. garlic salt
regular or horn-shaped corn
    chips

Place cream cheese in a large bowl. With an electric mixer on medium speed, gradually blend milk into cream cheese. Stir in shrimp. Add remaining ingredients except corn chips; stir until well mixed. Cover and chill for 2 hours. Serve with your favorite corn chips. Makes about 1-1/2 cups.

It's fun to hang little unexpected surprises from the dining room chandelier! Start with a swag of greenery, then tuck in Christmas whimsies like glass balls, tiny snowmen, cookie cutters and smiling Santas.

I'll Be Home for *Christmas* Cookbook

Savory Spinach Appetizer

Judy Phelan
Macomb, IL

A warm appetizer to serve when you're hosting family & friends.

1/4 c. butter, melted
3 eggs, beaten
1 c. milk
3/4 c. all-purpose flour
1 t. baking powder
1 t. salt
1/2 c. onion, chopped

1/2 c. mushrooms, chopped
3 c. finely shredded sharp
    Cheddar cheese
10-oz. pkg. frozen chopped
    spinach, thawed and well
    drained

Spread butter in a 13"x9" baking pan, coating bottom and sides of pan; set aside. In a large bowl, combine remaining ingredients; mix well and spoon into pan. Bake, uncovered, at 350 degrees for 35 minutes, or until lightly golden. Cool slightly; cut into squares. Makes 2-1/2 dozen.

For a fun party favor, add whimsical patterns and holiday greetings to plain glass ball ornaments with colorful glitter pens from the craft store. Or heap the makings in a basket so guests can make & take their own.

Christmas
Open House

Sausage Wonton Bites

Cheryl Harber
Schenectady, NY

I tried this recipe at our family Christmas Eve get-together years ago, and I fell in love with it. It's very rich, but out of this world!

16-oz. pkg. ground pork sausage
24 wonton wrappers
1 c. ranch salad dressing
1 c. shredded Monterey Jack
   cheese

1 c. shredded sharp Cheddar
   cheese
Optional: 1 to 2 T. canned diced
   green chiles

In a skillet over medium heat, cook and break up sausage; drain. Meanwhile, press wrappers gently into ungreased mini muffin cups. Bake at 350 degrees for 5 minutes; let cool. Stir remaining ingredients into sausage; spoon into wonton cups. Bake at 350 degrees for 15 minutes, or until bubbly and golden. Makes 2 dozen.

Bacon-Stuffed Mushrooms

Dale Driggers
Lexington, SC

These yummy tidbits disappear the minute I put them on the table. A requested dish everywhere I go!

8-oz. pkg. cream cheese,
   softened
1/2 lb. bacon, crisply cooked
   and crumbled

1/4 t. garlic powder
2 lbs. whole button mushrooms,
   stems removed

In a bowl, mix together cream cheese, bacon and garlic powder until well blended. Spoon mixture into mushroom caps; place on a baking sheet sprayed with non-stick vegetable spray. Bake at 400 degrees for 15 to 20 minutes, until lightly golden and heated through. Serve warm. Makes 12 servings.

Don't toss those leftover mushroom stems...chop them for a delicious addition to omelets.

Chicken Ranch Dip

Nancy Lanning
Lancaster, SC

Recently I made this dip for a Christmas party, adding cranberries and pecans to a recipe I already had. It was definitely a hit! Some dipper ideas...crackers, pretzels, carrot and celery sticks. The dip is pretty thick, so make sure your dippers are sturdy!

2 8-oz. pkgs. cream cheese, room temperature
12-1/2 oz. can chicken, drained and flaked
1 c. shredded Cheddar cheese
1-oz. pkg. ranch salad dressing mix
1 c. sweetened dried cranberries
1 c. chopped pecans

Combine all ingredients together in a large bowl; blend well. Cover and refrigerate until serving time. Makes 20 servings.

Special Raspberry Punch

Carolyn Deckard
Bedford, IN

This is a great punch recipe. Mom always made it at Christmas. We have enjoyed it at lots of family parties over the years.

4 10-oz. pkgs. frozen raspberries, thawed and juice reserved
6-oz. can frozen lemonade concentrate, thawed
2-ltr. bottle ginger ale, chilled

In a large saucepan over medium heat, cook raspberries with juice for 10 minutes, stirring often; cool slightly. Push berries through a strainer with a large spoon to remove seeds, reserving the juice. Discard seeds and pulp. Refrigerate raspberry juice at least 2 hours. In a punch bowl or large pitcher, combine raspberry juice and lemonade concentrate; stir in ginger ale. Serve immediately over ice. Makes 24 servings.

Christmas
Open House

Barn Party Spread

Bernadette Arndt
Ruma, IL

I shared this appetizer when my friends had a "Christmas in the Barn" party. It was a memorable night of live music, food and friendship. The guests all seemed to enjoy this spread!

2 8-oz. pkgs. cream cheese,
    room temperature
4 t. taco seasoning mix

1/2 red pepper, finely diced
2-1/4 oz. pkg. real bacon bits
round buttery crackers

In a large bowl, blend cream cheese and taco seasoning; fold in red pepper and bacon bits. Mound mixture onto a serving plate and round smoothly. Serve immediately, or cover and refrigerate. Serve with crackers. Serves 12.

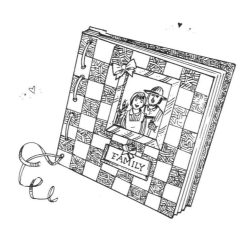

When you have family members visiting for the holidays, get out the old picture albums and family films. What a joy to reminisce together, laugh and share special memories of childhood and Christmases past!

Homemade Salami

*Elizabeth Smithson
Mayfield, KY*

*When Christmas parties roll around, everyone wants me to
make this! Granny always had it at least once during the holidays.
It's delicious served with cheese and crackers.*

2 lbs. lean ground beef chuck
1/2 c. water
2 T. curing salt
1 T. mustard seed

1 t. coarse pepper
1/2 t. smoke-flavored
   cooking sauce
1/4 t. onion powder

In a large bowl, mix all ingredients well. Form tightly into 3 to 5 log-shaped rolls, about 2 inches thick. Wrap separately in aluminum foil; refrigerate for 24 hours. Unwrap; place rolls on wire racks set in rimmed baking sheets. Bake at 350 degrees for 50 minutes. Turn halfway over; bake another 50 minutes. Cool slightly and slice. Serves 16.

Aunt Katie's Salami Roll-Ups

*Stephanie D'Esposito
Ravena, NY*

*These easy-to-make snacks are so delicious and flavorful,
no one can eat just one!*

1 lb. sliced Genoa salami
7-1/2 oz. container plain, chive
   & onion or jalapeño cream
   cheese spread

1 to 2 16-oz. jars banana
   peppers, drained

Spread each salami slice with a little cream cheese. Put a pepper on top; roll it up and serve. Makes 12 servings.

Take dessert outside 'round a
wintry bonfire. Make s'mores
and memories!

Christmas
Open House

Beckie's Black-Eyed Pea Dip

Beckie Apple
Grannis, AR

I love having friends over and making unique foods to serve them. This yummy dip is always a hit! I like to serve it as an appetizer with tortilla chips or crispy crackers. It's great year 'round, but it always adds a little something different for special occasions. It can be prepared several days in advance, to be ready for those busy times.

2 16-oz. cans black-eyed
   peas, drained
15-1/2 oz. can yellow hominy,
   drained
6-oz. can sliced mushrooms,
   drained
4-oz. can diced green chiles
1 ripe tomato, chopped

3 green onions, diced
Optional: 1 jalapeño pepper,
   seeded and diced
1/4 c. zesty Italian salad dressing
2 T. hot pepper sauce
1/4 t. garlic powder
1/4 t. seasoned salt
1/4 t. pepper

Combine all ingredients in a large bowl; mix well. Cover and chill for 2 hours before serving. Makes 4 cups.

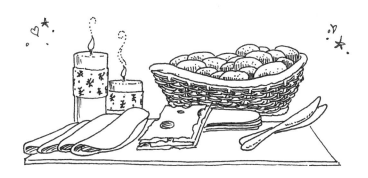

For an oh-so-easy gathering, serve up a festive sandwich buffet. Set out a savory selection of deli meats, cheeses, slider buns and other fixin's for make-your-own-sandwiches...yummy!

Creamy Salsa Dip

Carolyn Deckard
Bedford, IN

A friend brings this dip to our house every New Year's Eve.
It is so simple to make and everyone likes it.

1/2 c. sour cream
1/2 c. mayonnaise
3/4 c. chipotle salsa or chunky
   medium salsa

1/4 c. fresh cilantro, chopped
   and lightly packed
tortilla chips or sliced vegetables

In a small bowl, combine sour cream, mayonnaise, salsa and cilantro; mix well. Serve immediately with tortilla chips or vegetables, or cover and refrigerate one to 2 hours to blend flavors. Makes 2 cups.

Crock Queso Dip

Krista Marshall
Fort Wayne, IN

I've been making this for years for Sunday football viewing at our house. It's also perfect for parties, because it never seems to end!

32-oz. pkg. pasteurized process
   cheese, cubed
8-oz. pkg. cream cheese,
   softened
10-3/4 oz. can cream of
   mushroom soup

10-oz. can diced tomatoes with
   green chiles
1 lb. ground pork sausage,
   browned and drained

In a 4-quart slow cooker, combine cheeses and soup; stir well. Add tomatoes; mix again. Cover and cook on low setting for 30 minutes. Add sausage and stir well. Cover and cook on low setting for another 30 minutes, stirring occasionally, or until cheeses are completely melted and combined. For serving, turn slow cooker to warm (or off). If dip becomes too thick, add a few splashes of water to thin it out. Serves 10 or more.

Christmas
Open House

Warm French Onion Dip

Gina Taylor
Stroudsburg, PA

I first tasted this at a housewarming party several years ago, and it has become my go-to party dip. So simple and delicious.

10-3/4 oz. can French
  onion soup
8-oz. pkg. cream cheese,
  softened

1 c. shredded mozzarella cheese
sliced bread, snack crackers,
  sliced vegetables

In a bowl, blend soup and cream cheese until smooth; stir in mozzarella cheese. Spread into a lightly greased shallow one-quart casserole dish. Bake, uncovered, at 350 degrees for 30 minutes, or until bubbly and cheese is melted. Serve with bread, crackers or vegetables, as desired. Serves 8.

Tex-Mex Dip

Janet Haynes
Bowling Green, KY

This tried & true recipe was given to me by a good friend. It's delicious and different...I always bring home an empty dish. Serve with tortilla or corn chips. This recipe is easily halved for a smaller crowd.

2 8-oz. pkgs. cream cheese,
  softened

16-oz. jar picante sauce
2 c. shredded Cheddar cheese

In a large bowl, use a fork to mix cream cheese with picante sauce. Add shredded cheese and mix thoroughly. Spoon into a serving bowl; cover and chill. Serves 15 to 20.

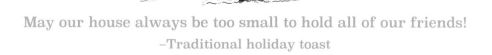

May our house always be too small to hold all of our friends!
–Traditional holiday toast

Hot Cranberry-Cider Drink

Heather Riley
Winterset, IA

When I was growing up, my mother used to make this recipe for holiday parties with friends and for Christmas Eve with the family. Now my own family enjoys it, and it just wouldn't be the Christmas season without it!

2 qts. apple cider
4 c. cranberry juice
2 c. orange juice
1 c. sugar

3 4-inch sticks whole cinnamon, broken
1 t. whole cloves
1 t. whole allspice

Add juices and sugar to a large coffeemaker. Place spices in the percolator basket and perk; serve hot. May also combine all ingredients in a stockpot; simmer over medium heat until hot and blended. Makes 15 to 20 servings.

Turn your holiday cards into a Christmas garland.... use mini clothespins to clip them to a length of ribbon. Add some favorite holiday photos to create a heartfelt decoration that your family will enjoy all season long.

Come In &
Warm Up!

Too-Busy-to-Cook Chili

Jill Ball
Highland, UT

With family parties, work parties, school plays, piano concerts, gift shopping, decorating and all the other hectic holiday activities, who has time to cook? Not me! So I like to find time one day and make a huge pot of chili. A triple batch of this recipe is just right! Then I freeze it in family-size portions to pull out on busy nights, for a hot, homemade meal in minutes.

1 lb. ground beef	1-1/2 c. water
1 onion, chopped	1/8 t. chili powder, or to taste
14-1/2 oz. can stewed tomatoes	1/8 t. garlic powder
15-oz. can tomato sauce	salt and pepper to taste
15-1/2 oz. can kidney beans	

In a large saucepan over medium heat, combine beef and onion. Cook until beef is browned and onion is tender; drain. Add tomatoes with juice and remaining ingredients. Stir well; bring to a boil. Reduce heat to low; cover and let simmer for 15 minutes. Serves 6.

Soups stay piping-hot when spooned into a slow cooker that's turned to the low setting. This way, no matter when guests arrive, the soup will be ready to enjoy.

Come In & Warm Up!

Cheddar Potato Soup

Lori Peterson
Effingham, KS

One Christmas Eve, my mother and I created this when we were snowed in. Mom was looking in my Gooseberry Patch *cookbooks for a soup recipe and the more she found, the more ideas she got. This was her end result!*

1 onion, diced
1/4 c. butter
6 c. potatoes, peeled and cubed
1 c. carrots, peeled and sliced
10-3/4 oz. can cream of
    chicken soup

8-oz. container sour cream
salt and pepper to taste
8-oz. pkg. Cheddar cheese,
    cubed

In a soup pot over medium heat, cook onion in butter until tender. Add potatoes, carrots and just enough water to cover. Bring to a boil; reduce heat to medium-low and cook until vegetables are tender. Add remaining ingredients; do not drain. Simmer over medium-low heat, stirring occasionally, until cheese is all melted. Makes 6 to 8 servings.

Vintage holiday aprons are practical and adorable! Look for the 1960s style with poinsettias, snowmen and Santa Claus...perfect gifts for friends who love to cook.

I'll Be Home for *Christmas* Cookbook

Slow-Cooker Corn Chowder

Sharon Nunn
Mechanicsville, VA

This is a creamy, comforting soup that I like to make for my family or to share with someone who has been in the hospital, had a new baby, etc. It's always well received. Serve with crusty bread or rolls.

3 c. milk
15-1/4 oz. can corn, drained
14-3/4 oz. can creamed corn
10-3/4 oz. can cream of
    mushroom soup

1 c. frozen shredded hashbrowns
1 c. cooked ham, cubed
1 onion, diced
2 T. butter
salt and pepper to taste

Combine all ingredients in a 3-quart slow cooker; stir well. Cover and cook on low setting for 5 to 6 hours. Makes 6 to 8 servings.

Best-Ever Cornbread

Sandy Ann Ward
Anderson, IN

Perfect with hot soup of all kinds!

2 8-1/2 oz. pkgs. corn
    muffin mix
2 eggs, beaten

1/3 c. sugar
2/3 c. whipping cream

In a large bowl, mix together all ingredients. Pour batter into a greased 13"x9" baking pan. Bake at 400 degrees for 20 to 25 minutes, until golden. Do not overbake. Makes 8 to 12 servings.

Take time for your town's special holiday events. Whether it's a Christmas parade, Santa arriving by horse-drawn sleigh or a tree lighting ceremony, hometown traditions make the best memories!

Come In & Warm Up!

Alice's Hamburger Stew

JoAlice Patterson-Welton
Lawrenceville, GA

I got this recipe from my late Mom. It is a family favorite, especially on cold winter or chilly fall evenings. An easy meal to prepare! Serve with cornbread for a tasty meal.

1 lb. ground beef chuck
1 c. onion, chopped
2 T. olive oil
4 c. carrots, peeled and sliced
   1-inch thick
4 c. water, divided

5 c. baking potatoes, peeled and
   cut into 1-inch cubes
3 T. tomato paste
1 t. salt
1/2 t. pepper

In a large skillet over medium heat, brown beef with onion in oil. Drain well; set aside. Meanwhile, in a Dutch oven over medium heat, combine carrots and 2 cups water. Bring to a boil; cook for 5 minutes. Add potatoes and remaining water; cook until vegetables are fork-tender. Add beef mixture, tomato paste and seasonings. Simmer for 15 minutes. Serves 12.

Cream Cheese Biscuits

Zoe Bennett
Columbia, SC

We love these oh-so-easy biscuits warm, spread with plenty of butter! To save time, just cut the dough into 12 squares.

2-1/2 c. biscuit baking mix
1/4 c. cream cheese, chilled

2 T. butter, chilled
3/4 c. milk

Add baking mix to a large bowl; use a fork to cut in cream cheese and butter. Add milk; stir just until combined. Knead dough 2 to 3 times on a floured surface. Roll out into a rectangle, 3/4-inch thick. Cut into 12 biscuits with a biscuit cutter; place on a parchment paper-lined baking sheet. Bake at 450 degrees for 10 to 12 minutes, until lightly golden. Makes one dozen.

Turkey Chili with Corn Dumplings

Vickie
Gooseberry Patch

My family loves chili and I've tried a lot of recipes. On a cold day, this one really hits the spot! If you don't have an oven-safe Dutch oven, prepare the chili in a soup pot, then transfer to a large casserole dish for baking.

2 t. oil
1 lb. Italian ground turkey
   sausage
1 c. onion, chopped
1 c. carrots, peeled and chopped
1-1/2 T. chili powder, or to taste
1 T. garlic, minced
1 t. ground cumin

1/2 t. salt
28-oz. can puréed tomatoes
15-1/2 oz. can black beans,
   drained and rinsed
4-oz. can diced green chiles
1 zucchini, thinly sliced
8-1/2 oz. pkg. corn muffin mix
3/4 c. green onions, thinly sliced

Heat oil in a Dutch oven. Add sausage, onion, carrots and seasonings; cook until sausage is no longer pink. Add tomatoes with juice, beans and chiles; simmer for 8 to 10 minutes, until slightly thickened. Remove from heat; stir in zucchini and transfer to oven. Bake, uncovered, at 400 degrees for 35 minutes, or until hot and bubbly around edges. Meanwhile, prepare muffin mix according to package directions, adding the green onions. Add batter to chili by large spoonfuls. Bake another 25 minutes, or until dumplings are cooked through and golden. Serves 6.

Spend a cozy evening in front of the fireplace, stringing popcorn and fresh cranberries to wind around the Christmas tree. Be sure to have some cookies to enjoy and hot cider to sip...memories in the making!

Come In & Warm Up!

Easy Taco Soup

Kathy Courington
Canton, GA

I made this slow-cooker soup for a church workday and everyone loved it, so I kept the recipe. Great for potlucks, as it makes a crockful of goodness. Very yummy and satisfying! Serve with tortilla chips or cornbread muffins.

2 lbs. ground beef, browned
   and drained
1 onion, diced
4 14-1/2 oz. cans diced tomatoes
15-oz. kidney beans
15-oz. pinto beans
15-1/4 oz. sweet corn & diced
   peppers, drained

4-oz. can diced green chiles,
   drained
1-oz. pkg. taco seasoning mix
1-oz. pkg. ranch salad dressing
   mix
Garnish: shredded cheese,
   sour cream

In a 6-quart slow cooker, combine all ingredients except garnish. Do not drain tomatoes or beans. Cover and cook on low setting for 6 to 8 hours. Serve topped with shredded cheese and sour cream. Makes 8 to 10 servings.

Oh, there's no place like home for the holidays,
'Cause no matter how far away you roam,
When you pine for the sunshine of a friendly gaze
For the holidays you can't beat home sweet home!

—Al Stillman

Italian Bean Soup

Joslyn Hornstrom
Elgin, IL

Whenever I want something warm and comforting, I turn to this quick soup. My mother got this recipe from our Italian landlady when I was five, I'm now 77. I've revised the recipe to use dried herbs and spices for when I don't have a lot of time to cook. Serve with additional Parmesan cheese and crusty bread...delicious!

8 c. chicken broth
2 15-1/2 oz. cans cannellini
   or Great Northern beans,
   drained and rinsed
15-oz. can tomato sauce
3 carrots, peeled and sliced
3 stalks celery, sliced
1 T. dried parsley

1-1/2 t. dried, minced onion
1-1/2 t. Italian seasoning
1 t. garlic powder
salt and pepper to taste
1-1/2 c. ditalini pasta, uncooked
1 c. fresh baby spinach
1/3 c. grated Parmesan cheese

In a large soup pot over high heat, bring broth to a boil. Stir in remaining ingredients except pasta, spinach and cheese. Return to a boil; reduce heat to medium. Cover and simmer for 20 minutes, or until carrots and celery are nearly tender. Stir in pasta and return to a boil; reduce heat to medium-low. Cover and simmer for 15 minutes longer, or until pasta is cooked. Stir in spinach and Parmesan cheese. Turn off heat; cover and let stand for 5 minutes. Serves 8 to 10.

Keep all of your family's favorite holiday story books in a basket by a cozy chair. Set aside one night as family night to read your favorites together.

Come In & Warm Up!

Mom's Hearty Lentil Soup

Lynda McCormick
Burkburnett, TX

I can recall my mom making this soup when I was a child, and my youngest brother sneaking the hot dogs out of the pot before it got to the table! She always served this in the wintertime with a loaf of crusty bread. A great recipe to double!

5 c. water
1 c. dried lentils, rinsed
   and sorted
1 bay leaf
1-1/2 t. salt
1/2 c. onion, diced

1 T. butter
14-1/2 oz. can diced tomatoes
1 carrot, peeled and diced
1 stalk celery, diced
1/8 t. dried thyme
3 to 4 hot dogs, sliced

In a soup pot over high heat, combine water, lentils, bay leaf and salt; bring to a boil. Reduce heat to medium and simmer until lentils are tender, 30 to 45 minutes. Discard bay leaf. Meanwhile, in a small skillet over medium heat, cook onion in butter until translucent. Add onion mixture to soup pot along with undrained tomatoes, carrots, celery and thyme. If a thinner consistency is desired, add more water as needed. Simmer another 15 minutes. Stir in hot dogs and cook another 5 minutes. Makes 4 to 6 servings.

It is good to be children sometimes,
and never better than at Christmas.

–Charles Dickens

Pepper Jack Potato Soup

Wanda Galloway
Superior, MT

A delicious hot soup for a cold winter day. Especially tasty with Cheddar bacon biscuits or a BLT sandwich...mmm good!

4 c. potatoes, peeled and diced
2 T. olive oil
1 green pepper, diced
1 red pepper, diced
2/3 c. yellow onion, diced
1 carrot, peeled and diced
2 cloves garlic, minced
2-1/2 c. chicken broth
3 slices bacon, crisply cooked
  and crumbled

1/3 c. half-and-half or milk
1 t. dried thyme
1/2 t. salt, or to taste
1/2 t. white pepper
1/2 c. butter
1/2 c. all-purpose flour
1 c. whipping cream
1 c. shredded Pepper Jack cheese
Optional: additional half-and-
  half or milk

In a soup pot over high heat, cover potatoes with water. Bring to a boil. Simmer about 15 minutes, until tender; drain. Meanwhile, heat oil in a skillet over medium heat. Add peppers, onion, carrot and garlic; sauté until vegetables are soft. Transfer vegetable mixture with broth to potatoes in soup pot; add crumbled bacon, half-and-half or milk and seasonings. In the same skillet, melt butter over medium heat; stir in flour to make a paste. Slowly add cream; cook and stir until bubbly, mixture thickens and comes away from sides of pan. Stir cream mixture and cheese into soup until cheese is melted. If desired, stir in a little more half-and-half or milk to desired consistency. Makes 6 servings.

Keep rolls toasty warm for serving with soup. Before arranging rolls in a bread basket, place a terra cotta warming tile in the bottom and line with a tea towel.

Come In & Warm Up!

Cheesy Tomato Soup

Dale Duncan
Waterloo, IA

*There's nothing like hot tomato soup to raise spirits
on a cold, wet day!*

4 French baguette slices
3 T. butter, softened and divided
1 onion, chopped
2 carrots, peeled and chopped
2 stalks celery, chopped
1 clove garlic, minced

28-oz. can crushed tomatoes
3 c. vegetable broth
1 t. salt
1/2 t. pepper
1/4 c. whipping cream
2 c. shredded Gruyère cheese

Spread baguette slices with 2 tablespoons butter; place on an ungreased baking sheet. Bake at 400 degrees for 2 to 3 minutes, until golden; set aside. Melt remaining butter in a large saucepan over medium heat. Add onion, carrots, celery and garlic; cook for 2 to 3 minutes, until tender. Stir in tomatoes with juice, broth and seasonings. Bring to a boil; reduce heat to medium-low and simmer for 15 minutes. Working in batches, carefully pour soup into a blender; process until smooth and return to saucepan. Stir in cream. Divide soup among 4 ovenproof soup bowls and set on a baking sheet. Top each bowl with a baguette slice and 1/2 cup cheese. Place under broiler and broil for 3 to 5 minutes, until cheese is melted and bubbly. Serves 4.

Top bowls of soup with crunchy cheese toasts. Thinly slice French bread and brush with olive oil. Broil for 2 to 3 minutes, until golden; turn over. Sprinkle with shredded Parmesan cheese and Italian seasoning. Broil another 2 to 3 minutes, until cheese melts. Yum!

Marta's Homemade Mushroom Soup

Marta Norton
Redlands, CA

So good on cold-weather days...or whenever the mood strikes! Use familiar white button mushrooms, or a mixture of mushrooms.

1/4 c. butter
2 lbs. mushrooms, chopped
3 cloves garlic, minced
3/4 c. onion, chopped
1 t. ground sage
1 c. white wine or chicken broth

4 c. chicken broth
1 c. whipping cream
1 c. grated Parmesan cheese
1/2 t. dried thyme
2 to 3 T. cornstarch
salt and pepper to taste

Melt butter in a large stockpot over medium heat; add mushrooms and garlic. Cook, stirring occasionally, for 5 to 6 minutes, until tender and golden. Stir in onion and sage. Cook, stirring often, until translucent, 2 to 3 minutes. Stir in one cup wine or broth; bring to a boil. Reduce heat and simmer for 5 minutes, or until slightly reduced. Transfer half to 2/3 of soup into a blender; process until smooth. Return soup to remaining soup in stockpot. Stir in broth, cream, Parmesan cheese and thyme. In a small bowl, combine 2 tablespoons cornstarch with 1/4 cup broth from stockpot; whisk until smooth. Stir cornstarch mixture into soup; simmer until slightly thickened. Season with salt and pepper. If soup is too thin, combine remaining cornstarch with 2 tablespoons broth from stockpot; add to soup and stir until desired consistency is reached. Makes 8 to 10 servings.

Wrapping up a slow cooker as a gift for newlyweds?
Jot down all your favorite, tried & true recipes and tuck 'em
inside. A thoughtful gift that's sure to be appreciated!

Come In & Warm Up!

Onion & Fontina Bread

Cindy Neel
Gooseberry Patch

*This savory bread isn't hard to make. It really dresses up
a bowl of soup or stew for dinner!*

1 c. onion, diced
1 T. olive oil
3 c. all-purpose flour
3 T. sugar
2 t. baking powder

1 t. salt
1 c. shredded fontina cheese
12-oz. bottle amber ale or
    non-alcoholic beer
1/4 c. butter, melted and divided

In a skillet over medium heat, cook onion in oil until tender, about
6 minutes. Remove from heat; cool to room temperature. In a large
bowl, combine flour, sugar, baking powder and salt; mix well and make
a well in the center. Add onion mixture, cheese and ale or beer to the
well; stir just until batter is moistened. Spoon batter into a greased
9"x5" loaf pan; drizzle with 2 tablespoons butter. Bake at 375 degrees
for 35 minutes. Brush remaining butter over loaf. Bake for another
20 to 23 minutes, until a toothpick inserted in center tests clean. Set
pan on a wire rack for 5 minutes; turn out loaf and cool completely on
rack. Makes one loaf.

Early in the holiday season, make a list of cookies to bake,
cards to write and gifts to buy. Even Santa makes a list!
Post it on the fridge...you'll be able to check off each item
with satisfaction as it's completed.

Mom's Cure-All Cabbage Soup

Allison Paschal
Bauxite, AR

Whenever we kids were sick, Mom would make this soup. We all thought we didn't like cabbage, kidney beans or tomatoes, but when this soup was served, we ate it up! Especially when paired with some buttered cornbread...yum!

1-1/2 lbs. lean ground beef
1 c. onion, chopped
2 T. oil
1 head cabbage, chopped
1 c. water
2 14-1/2 oz. cans diced tomatoes
46-oz. can vegetable cocktail
   juice
2 15-1/2 oz. cans kidney beans,
   drained
6-oz. can tomato paste
4-oz. can diced green chiles
2 1-oz. pkgs. Italian salad
   dressing mix
salt and pepper to taste

Brown beef in a skillet over medium heat; drain. Meanwhile, in a soup pot over medium heat, sauté onion in oil until tender. Add cabbage and water; simmer until cabbage is tender. Add browned beef, tomatoes with juice and remaining ingredients; stir well. Cover and bring to a boil. Turn heat to low and simmer for one hour, stirring occasionally. Makes 12 servings.

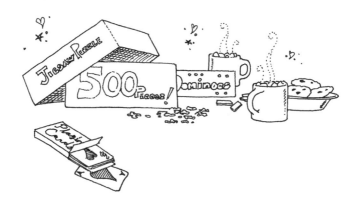

For snow-day fun, pull out jigsaw puzzles, nostalgic games like checkers and dominoes or card games like Go Fish.

Come In & Warm Up!

Best Chicken Noodle Soup

Liz Blackstone
Racine, WI

When I was growing up, at Christmas we'd visit my grandmother in the country, where we could skate on her frozen farm pond. When we came back inside with rosy cheeks and cold hands after skating, she always had a big kettle of her delicious chicken soup to warm us up. This recipe isn't hers, but I think it comes pretty close!

2 T. olive oil
1/2 c. onion, chopped
2 carrots, peeled and sliced
2 stalks celery, sliced
5 cloves garlic, chopped
8 c. chicken broth
2-1/2 lbs. chicken breasts
    and thighs, skin removed
    if desired

2-1/2 c. narrow egg noodles,
    uncooked
3 T. fresh parsley, chopped
2 T. fresh dill, chopped
2 T. lemon juice
salt and pepper to taste

Heat oil in a Dutch oven over medium heat. Add onion, carrots, celery and garlic. Cook for 8 to 10 minutes, stirring occasionally, until softened. Add broth and chicken pieces. Bring to a boil over high heat; reduce heat to low. Cover and simmer until chicken is cooked through, 40 to 45 minutes. Remove chicken to a platter; cool slightly. Cut breasts into bite-size pieces; shred thighs with 2 forks, discarding bones. Return chicken to soup; add noodles. Cook, stirring often, for 6 to 8 minutes, until tender. Stir in parsley, dill and lemon juice; season with salt and pepper. Serves 8.

Soup to go! Tuck a big jar of Best Chicken Noodle Soup, a packet of saltines and a cheery soup bowl into a basket. Sure to be equally appreciated by a friend with the sniffles or one who simply doesn't get enough homemade meals!

Hearty Fish Chowder

Mia Rossi
Charlotte, NC

This savory chowder was one of the seven fish dishes my family shared on Christmas Eve. It's delicious anytime, though!

2 T. olive oil	1-1/2 c. water
1/2 c. sweet onion, chopped	1 t. seafood seasoning
3 c. celery, chopped	1-1/2 t. salt
2 carrots, peeled and grated	1/2 t. pepper
1 to 2 potatoes, peeled and diced	1 lb. grouper or tilapia fillets,
1 to 2 leeks, chopped	cut into large cubes
1 clove garlic, minced	1 c. half-and-half
14-oz. can chicken broth	Garnish: butter, oyster crackers

Heat oil in a soup pot over medium heat. Sauté onion for 5 minutes, or until tender. Add celery, carrots, potatoes, leeks and garlic. Cook for 7 minutes, stirring occasionally. Add broth, water and seasonings; bring to a boil. Reduce heat to medium-low; cover and simmer for 30 minutes. Add fish; cover and simmer for 20 minutes. Stir in half-and-half; heat through but do not boil. Top each bowl with a pat of butter; serve with oyster crackers. Makes 8 servings.

Oyster Soup

Shirley Parsons
Eskridge, KS

A tradition on Christmas Eve...serve in small bowls.

1/2 gal. whole milk	3 8-oz. cans oysters
1/2 c. butter, sliced	salt and pepper to taste

Heat milk in a large saucepan over medium-low heat until warmed through. Add butter and oysters with juice. Simmer over low heat for 30 to 40 minutes; do not boil. Season with salt and pepper. Keep warm over low heat. Makes 10 to 12 servings.

Tie ornaments onto the tree with narrow strips of homespun fabric... sweet and simple!

Come In & Warm Up!

Salmon Chowder

Sharon Nunn
Mechanicsville, VA

My mom makes this yummy chowder, and I've always loved it. This is my version. Any mild white fish can be substituted for the salmon, and you can use almond milk with good results.

1/4 c. butter
1 c. onion, diced
1 stalk celery, diced
1 lb. potatoes, peeled and cut
    into 1-inch cubes
6 c. water
14-3/4 oz. can pink salmon,
    drained, skin and bones
    discarded

2 c. milk
salt and pepper to taste
Garnish: saltine or oyster
    crackers

Melt butter in a large soup pot over medium heat. Add onion and celery; sauté until soft. Add potatoes and water; stir. Bring to a boil; reduce heat to medium-low. Simmer for about 20 minutes, until potatoes are tender. Add salmon and heat through; slowly stir in milk. Season with salt and pepper. Cook and stir over low heat until heated through. Serve with crackers. Serves 4.

Mix old and new Santa decorations for a quick centerpiece... just arrange them in the center of a pine wreath. Oh-so easy!

Mac & Cheese Soup

Cyndy DeStefano
Hermitage, PA

In the wintertime, we love hot soup...we love macaroni & cheese too. One day after riding sleds, my son had friends over and so I needed to make the macaroni & cheese stretch a little further. So I combined the two, for a warm hearty meal that kids ask for, over & over.

9 c. water, divided
14-oz. pkg. deluxe macaroni & cheese dinner mix
1 c. broccoli, cut into bite-size flowerets
2 T. onion, finely chopped

10-3/4 oz. can Cheddar cheese soup or cream of broccoli soup
2-1/2 c. milk
2 c. cooked ham, diced

In a large saucepan over high heat, bring 8 cups water to a boil. Add macaroni, setting aside cheese sauce packet. Cook for 8 to 10 minutes, until tender. Meanwhile, in another large saucepan, bring remaining water to a boil. Add broccoli and onion; cook for 3 minutes. Stir in soup, milk, ham and contents of cheese sauce packet; heat through. Drain macaroni and stir into soup. Makes 8 servings.

Make spirits bright by stitching pompoms onto plain winter hats, scarves and mittens. Super-easy to do with just a needle and thread!

Come In & Warm Up!

Cabbage Patch Stew

Melissa Hutchens
New Hope, AL

My best friend Jane gave this recipe to me nearly 50 years ago and it's still a big hit today. In the fall and winter, it's so good with cornbread, crackers and grilled cheese sandwiches. Hope you and your family enjoy this simple recipe as much as we have.

1 to 2 lbs. ground beef
1/2 onion, chopped
salt and pepper to taste
1 head cabbage, chopped

28-oz. can crushed tomatoes
2 16-oz. cans pinto beans,
    drained and rinsed

In a soup pot over medium heat, brown beef with onion. Drain; season with salt and pepper. Add remaining ingredients and enough water to make a soupy consistency. Simmer over medium-low heat for one hour or longer, stirring occasionally. Makes 10 to 15 servings.

Potato-Bacon Soup

Susan Church
Holly, MI

Great on a cold day...really warms you through & through!

2 slices bacon, diced
1 onion, chopped
5 potatoes, peeled and cubed

16-oz. container half-and-half
1 t. salt

In a large saucepan over medium heat, cook bacon until crisp. Remove bacon with a slotted spoon, reserving drippings in pan. Add onion and cook until golden. Add potatoes and enough water to cover potatoes. Simmer for 30 minutes; do not drain. Reduce heat to low; stir in half-and-half and salt. Cover and simmer for another 30 minutes, stirring occasionally. Serves 8.

Pass on holiday spirit with a good winter deed! Shovel the driveway and sidewalk for a neighbor.

Christmas Ham Soup

Amanda Walton
Marysville, OH

This yummy soup is super filling and comforting on a cold winter day, as well as being a great way to use up some of that leftover Christmas ham!

1 c. onion, chopped
1 c. celery, chopped
1 c. carrot, peeled and chopped
3 T. butter
1 T. garlic, minced
8 c. chicken broth
1/2 c. milk
1/2 c. sour cream
1-oz. pkg. ranch salad
   dressing mix

1 t. dried thyme
salt and pepper to taste
8-oz. pkg. cream cheese, cubed
1 lb. potatoes, peeled and diced,
   or frozen diced potatoes
3 c broccoli, cut into bite-size
   flowerets
1 lb. cooked ham, diced

In a large stockpot over medium heat, sauté onion, celery and carrot in butter for 5 minutes. Add garlic and cook another 2 minutes. Add broth, milk and sour cream; bring to a gentle boil. Stir in dressing mix and seasonings. Add cream cheese; cook and stir until completely melted. Add potatoes; cook for 5 minutes. Add broccoli and ham; continue to cook until potatoes are fork-tender. Makes 6 to 8 servings.

When boxing up gifts to mail, try something new. Air-popped popcorn, the Sunday funnies and crumpled wrapping paper are all terrific ideas for filler...and much more fun than foam peanuts!

Come In & Warm Up!

Slow-Cooked Ham & Beans

Nancy Wise
Little Rock, AR

Who doesn't love a warm bowl of ham & beans, with a chunk of cornbread? Pure comfort, and so easy.

16-oz. pkg. dried Great Northern
    beans, rinsed and sorted
1 lb. ham bone or hocks
6 c. water

2 t. onion powder
pepper to taste
salt to taste

Combine all ingredients except salt in a 5-quart slow cooker; stir well. Cover and cook on low setting for 8 hours, or until beans are tender. Remove ham bone; slice off the meat and return to slow cooker. Season with salt. Serves 10 to 12.

Green Onion Rolls

Rowena Saunders
Newfoundland, Canada

These savory rolls are delicious...perfect with a hearty soup or your favorite pasta dish.

1-1/2 c. green onions, sliced
1 T. butter
1-lb. loaf frozen bread dough,
    thawed
1/3 c. grated Parmesan cheese

1/2 c. shredded mozzarella
    cheese
1/2 t. pepper
Optional: 3/4 t. garlic salt

In a small skillet, sauté onions in butter; set aside. On a floured surface, roll out dough into a 12-inch by 8-inch rectangle. Spread onion mixture over dough; sprinkle with cheeses, pepper and garlic salt, if desired. Roll up jelly-roll style, starting on one long side; pinch seams to seal. Cut into 12 slices; place each slice in a greased muffin cup. Cover and let rise in a warm place until doubled. Bake at 375 degrees for 18 to 20 minutes, until golden. Cool rolls on a wire rack. Makes one dozen.

White Chicken Chili

Kristi Root
Nashville, OH

This slow-cooker recipe is a family favorite on cold, chilly nights! It's a great meal to use up leftover chicken or turkey, along with the ease of coming home to a meal that's ready to serve. Just pair a tossed salad with it and your meal is complete.

2 lbs. boneless, skinless chicken
    breasts, cooked and cubed
4-1/2 c. chicken broth
2 15-1/2 oz. cans white kidney
    beans, drained and rinsed
15-oz. can garbanzo beans,
    drained and rinsed
4-oz. can chopped green chiles
1-1/2 c. onions, diced

2 cloves garlic, minced
1 T. canola oil
1 T. dried oregano
2 t. ground cumin
1-1/2 t. seasoned salt
1/4 t. cayenne pepper
Garnish: shredded Monterey Jack
    cheese, sour cream, salsa,
    tortilla chips

In a 5-quart slow cooker, combine all ingredients except garnish. Stir gently. Cover and cook on low setting for 6 to 8 hours. Serve with desired toppings. Makes 4 to 6 servings.

On baking days, pop an easy dinner in the slow cooker
first thing in the morning. Then relax and enjoy baking...
dinner will be ready whenever you are.

Come In & Warm Up!

Pork & Black Bean Chili

Marlene Burns
Swisher, IA

This is very good chili, my dad's favorite. It's easily made in a slow cooker. Add some cornbread and dinner is served!

1 T. canola oil
1-1/2 lbs. pork loin roast,
   cut into 1-inch cubes
2 cloves garlic, minced
1 T. chili powder
1/2 t. ground cumin

1/4 t. salt
2 14-1/2 oz. cans diced tomatoes
15-oz. can black beans, drained
   and rinsed
1 c. frozen corn
8-oz. can tomato sauce

Heat oil in a skillet over medium heat. Add pork, garlic and seasonings; cook until pork is browned. Transfer pork mixture to a 5-quart slow cooker. Add tomatoes with juice and remaining ingredients; stir gently. Cover and cook on low setting for 5 hours. Serves 4.

Spicy Cheddar Cornbread

Sarah Buschynski
Fort Edward, NY

Great for dunking into chili! This recipe is so tasty, I almost always have to make a double batch. It's so quick & easy to toss together. If you like more spice, add more green chiles, less if you don't.

8-1/2 oz. pkg. corn muffin mix
1/3 c. whole milk
1 egg, beaten
1/4 c. plus 2 T. butter, melted
   and divided

4-oz. can diced green chiles,
   well drained
1-1/2 c. shredded sharp Cheddar
   cheese, divided

In a large bowl, combine muffin mix, milk, egg and 1/4 cup melted butter; stir well. Add chiles and one cup cheese; mix well. Batter will be lumpy and thick. Pour batter into a greased 9"x9" baking pan. Bake at 375 degrees for 15 minutes. Drizzle with remaining butter; sprinkle with remaining cheese. Return to oven for 5 minutes, or until golden and cheese is melted. Serves 6.

I'll Be Home for
Christmas
Cookbook

Diane's Ground Beef Stew

Renée Davis
Alexander City, AL

This recipe has became a family favorite. I named it after my cousin Diane, who shared it with me. The best part is, there's no slicing, dicing or chopping required. Just open the cans, simmer and enjoy! My favorite alternative to ground beef is frozen mini meatballs.

2 lbs. ground beef
15-1/2 oz. can chili with beans
15-oz. can mixed vegetables
15-oz. can diced potatoes
14-1/2 oz. can diced tomatoes
   with green chiles

14-1/2 oz. can seasoned
   diced tomatoes
10-3/4 oz. vegetable beef soup
10-3/4 oz. can tomato soup
2 8-oz. cans tomato sauce
1 T. butter

In a large soup pot, brown beef over medium heat; drain. Add remaining ingredients; do not drain any cans. Stir well. Simmer over low heat for 2 hours, stirring occasionally. Serves 6 to 8.

Easy Garlic Knots

Jill Valentine
Jackson, TN

A fun change from ordinary rolls! These are great with soup or pasta. Use a pizza cutter to cut the dough...let the kids help!

13-oz. can refrigerated pizza
   dough
5 T. butter, melted
3 T. grated Parmesan cheese

1 t. dried parsley
1/2 t. garlic powder
1/2 t. dried oregano

Unroll dough; slice crosswise into 12 equal strips. Loosely tie strips into a knot shape, tucking the ends underneath. Arrange on a lightly greased baking sheet; set aside. In a small bowl, combine remaining ingredients. Brush butter mixture over rolls, reserving 1-1/2 tablespoons of mixture. Bake at 400 degrees for 10 to 12 minutes, until golden. Brush with reserved butter mixture. Makes one dozen.

Come In & Warm Up!

Creamy Wild Rice Chicken Soup

Betty Kozlowski
Newnan, GA

We love soups at our house, no matter the season! This slow-cooker recipe has become a family favorite. Very comforting on a chilly day.

5 c. water
6-oz. pkg. chicken-flavored
   long-grain & wild rice mix
10-3/4 oz. can cream of
   mushroom soup
4-oz. can sliced mushrooms,
   drained

1/2 t. dried thyme
1/4 t. pepper
1 c. cooked chicken, cubed
10-oz. pkg. frozen chopped
   spinach or kale, thawed

In a 5-quart slow cooker, combine all ingredients except chicken and spinach or kale; stir. Cover and cook on low setting for 7 to 8 hours, or on high setting for 3-1/2 to 4 hours. Stir in chicken and spinach or kale. Cover and continue cooking until heated through, 10 to 20 minutes. Makes 6 servings.

Variation: For a heartier soup with a richer broth, use 2 to 4 pieces of uncooked bone-in chicken, adding it at the beginning. Cook as directed. Remove chicken when cooked through. Stir in spinach as directed; chop or shred chicken and return to soup.

As much fun as when you were a kid...buy new jammies for everyone spending Christmas Eve at your home!

Best Broccoli & Cheese Soup

Teresa Eller
Kansas City, KS

This soup is so good on a cold winter's day. I serve it with grilled cheese sandwiches...sprinkle garlic powder on the buttered side of the bread and use process cheese. Yummo!

8 c. water
6 cubes chicken bouillon
1/2 c. onion, diced
1 t. garlic powder
1 t. celery salt
1 russet potato, peeled and diced
2 carrots, peeled and diced
1/2 c. celery, diced

1 c. broccoli, finely chopped
12-oz. can chicken, drained
and flaked
1 c. pasteurized process cheese,
cubed
2 c. half-and-half or whole milk
1/2 c. all-purpose flour

In a soup pot over high heat, bring water to a boil. Add bouillon cubes, onion, garlic powder and celery salt; simmer for 5 minutes. Add potato, carrots and celery; simmer for about 10 minutes, until vegetables are tender. Stir in broccoli and cook another 5 minutes; stir in chicken and cheese. In a shaker jar, combine half-and-half or milk and flour; shake well until flour dissolves. Add mixture to simmering soup; cook and stir until thickened. Serves 4.

Bake your own bread bowls! Thaw a loaf of frozen bread dough and cut into 2 or 3 pieces. Arrange on baking sheets sprayed with non-stick vegetable spray; cover with sprayed plastic wrap. Let rise until double in size. Uncover; bake at 350 degrees for 25 minutes, or until golden. Cool, slice off tops and hollow out...ready to fill with soup!

Come In & Warm Up!

Hearty Lasagna Soup

Rhonda Hauenstein
Tell City, IN

This has become one of the most popular soups with my family. We love lasagna...this soup is quicker to make and tastes just as good!

1 lb. ground beef or turkey
3/4 c. onion, chopped
2 14-oz. cans beef broth
14-1/2 oz. can Italian-seasoned
   diced tomatoes
1 c. water
1/4 t. garlic powder

1/2 t. Italian seasoning
2 c. corkscrew pasta or other
   small pasta, uncooked
1/4 c. grated Parmesan cheese
Optional: additional Parmesan
   cheese

In a soup pot over medium heat, cook beef or turkey with onion until browned; drain. Add broth, tomatoes with juice, water and seasonings; bring to a boil. Stir in pasta; cook over medium heat for 8 to 10 minutes, until pasta is tender. Stir in cheese. Serve with additional cheese, if desired. Makes 8 servings.

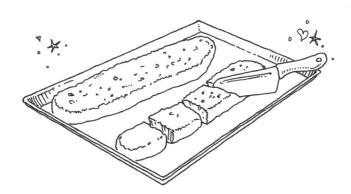

Hot garlic bread can't be beat! Mix 1/2 cup melted butter and 2 teaspoons minced garlic; spread over a split loaf of Italian bread. Sprinkle with chopped fresh parsley. Bake at 350 degrees for 8 minutes, or until hot, then broil briefly, until golden. Cut into generous slices.

One-Hour Buttermilk Rolls

Pam Hooley
LaGrange, IN

I got this recipe from a friend in New Mexico, when we were first married and serving a year of voluntary service for the church. That was over 40 years ago, and it's still a wonderful standby, easy and quick. You can make this dough into dinner rolls, or roll it into cinnamon rolls...works well for either!

2 envs. active dry yeast	1-1/2 c. buttermilk, warmed
1/4 c. very warm water,	4-1/2 c. all-purpose flour
110 to 115 degrees	1/2 t. baking soda
3 T. sugar	1 t. salt
1/2 c. oil or melted shortening	Optional: softened butter

In a large bowl, add yeast to warm water; stir in sugar and oil or shortening. Let stand several minutes. Add remaining ingredients except optional butter. With an electric mixer on medium speed, or by hand, beat until dough is smooth. Cover with a tea towel and let rise in a warm place for 10 minutes. Shape into 12 rolls; arrange rolls on a lightly greased baking sheet. Cover again; let rise another 30 minutes. Bake at 400 degrees for 15 to 20 minutes. If desired, brush rolls with softened butter as soon as they come out of the oven. Makes one dozen.

Pile everyone into the car and head to the local cut-your-own tree farm. There's almost always creamy cocoa and snacks to share, and sometimes, even a surprise visit from Santa & Mrs. Claus!

Come In & Warm Up!

2-Way Snack Crackers

Kathy Grashoff
Fort Wayne, IN

Oh my goodness, are these ever good! You use two types of crackers, which is a little different. Serve them in little baskets lined with a napkin...they will be gobbled up!

1/2 c. oil
1-oz. pkg. ranch dressing mix
4 c. oyster crackers

2 c. bite-sized Cheddar cheese crackers

Whisk together oil and dressing mix in a large bowl. Add crackers, tossing to coat. Spread crackers in a single layer on lightly greased baking sheets. Bake at 350 degrees for 15 minutes, stirring after 7 minutes. Let cool on wax paper in a single layer. Store in an airtight container at room temperature. Makes 6 cups.

Dilly Onion Oyster Crackers

Jill Burton
Gooseberry Patch

For soups and snacking, these crackers can't be beat!

12-oz. pkg. oyster crackers
1/4 c. olive oil

1-1/2 T. onion soup mix
1-1/2 t. dried dill weed

Pour crackers into a large bowl; set aside. Combine oil, soup mix and dill in a cup; pour over crackers and toss to coat. Spread crackers in a single layer on an ungreased large baking sheet. Bake at 250 degrees for 15 to 20 minutes. Cool; store in an airtight container. Makes 8 cups.

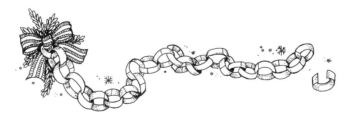

Make memories with a little one by creating a simple paper chain...decorate the tree or count down to the big day with each loop!

Hoppin' John Soup

Sandy Coffey
Cincinnati, OH

This is something I came up with...a soup version of this classic New Year's Day dish. Eat it for good luck!

4 c. water
1/2 c. long-cooking brown
  rice, uncooked
3 cubes chicken bouillon
1 t. chili powder

1 green pepper, diced
1 onion, diced
16-oz. can black-eyed peas,
  drained
2 c. cooked ham, cubed

In a Dutch oven over high heat, combine water, rice, bouillon cubes and chili powder; bring to a boil. Add green pepper, onion, peas and ham. Reduce heat to medium-low. Cover and simmer for 30 to 40 minutes, until vegetables and rice are tender. Serves 4 to 6.

Fizzy Soda Biscuits

Ann Tober
Biscoe, AR

For really good rolls, this is the easiest recipe ever! Everyone thinks they take a lot of time, but they don't.

2 c. biscuit baking mix
1/2 c. sour cream

1/2 c. lemon-lime soda
1/4 c. butter, melted

Place biscuit mix in a large bowl; cut in sour cream. Add soda; stir until a very soft dough forms. Sprinkle a little extra biscuit mix on counter; pat dough out and cut with a biscuit cutter. Spread melted butter in an 8"x8" baking pan; arrange biscuits in pan. Bake at 450 degrees for 12 to 15 minutes, until golden. Makes one dozen.

A sweet keepsake for a family get-together. Copy a favorite family recipe onto a festive card, then punch a hole in the corner and tie the card to a rolled napkin with a length of ribbon.

Come In & Warm Up!

Lentil Mushroom Soup

Shirley Howie
Foxboro, MA

This is a hearty meatless soup that I make often, usually at my husband's request. It's simple in a slow cooker. I like to serve it with warm rolls and butter. Nothing else needed...it's a meal in itself!

2 cubes beef or vegetable
   bouillon
3 c. boiling water
10-3/4 oz. can cream of
   mushroom soup
1 c. dried lentils, rinsed
   and sorted

2 to 3 carrots, peeled and
   thinly sliced
3/4 c. onion, chopped
1 c. celery, sliced
1 T. dried parsley

In a bowl, dissolve bouillon cubes in boiling water. Add soup; stir until well mixed. In a 4-quart slow cooker, combine remaining ingredients. Add bouillon mixture; stir to combine well. Cover and cook on low setting for 8 to 10 hours, or on high setting for 5 to 6 hours. Makes 4 servings.

If the kids just can't wait 'til Christmas, celebrate early on Saint Nicholas Day, December 6th. Each child sets out their shoes the night before. Old Saint Nick fills the shoes of those who've behaved with treats and small presents...such fun!

Farmhouse Creamy Chicken & Vegetable Soup

Sacha George
Kalamazoo, MI

I have fond memories of spending time at home during the holidays, with a bowl of hot soup after sledding. Serve with a grilled cheese sandwich made with ciabatta bread...yum!

2 to 3 boneless, skinless chicken
   breasts, cubed
32-oz. container chicken broth
14-1/2 oz. can cream of
   chicken soup
2 c. frozen peas
2 c. carrots, peeled and chopped
2 c. potatoes, peeled and chopped

2 c. celery, chopped
1 onion, chopped
2 T. garlic, minced
1 to 2 t. dried rosemary
3 bay leaves
salt and pepper to taste
1/2 c. half-and-half

In a 6-quart slow cooker, combine all ingredients except half-and-half. Stir gently to mix. Cover and cook on low setting for 6 to 8 hours. In the last 30 minutes of cooking, discard bay leaves; stir in half-and-half. Serves 8 to 10.

Winter is a fun-filled, magical time of year...make snow angels, go sledding, even try ice skating! A wintry bonfire with food, family & friends will make it a time to remember.

Seasonal
Salads & Sides

Fennel & Citrus Salad

Toni Leathers
Claremont, CA

This delicious recipe is dear to my heart. My Noni made it all the time when I was a little girl, and as I got older, she let me make this salad for all our family gatherings. It brings back such fun-loving memories of my Noni. Mangia and enjoy!

1 fennel bulb, halved and cored
2 blood oranges or navel oranges
2 T. white wine vinegar
1 T. honey
1 t. salt

2 heads Bibb lettuce, torn into
  bite-size pieces
1 Gala apple, cored and diced
1/4 c. olive oil

Use a mandolin or a sharp knife to shave fennel bulb into thin slices. Chop 2 tablespoons fennel fronds; set aside. Use a zester or grater to grate 2 tablespoons zest from oranges; set zest aside. Peel and section oranges. Squeeze half of one orange section into a serving bowl; discard orange section. Add fennel with fronds, vinegar, honey and salt; mix gently. Let stand for about 30 minutes. Shortly before serving time, add remaining orange sections, lettuce, apple and olive oil; toss gently. Serves 6.

Candy cane-style napkin rings are child's play to make!
Twist together fluffy red and white pipe cleaners and
slip napkins inside.

Seasonal
Salads & Sides

John's Favorite Salad

Beverley Williams
San Antonio, TX

I made this salad during the holidays. My autistic son John ate four helpings...I had to make another bowl of salad!

2 c. romaine lettuce, torn into
    bite-size pieces
2 c. fresh spinach, torn into
    bite-size pieces
2 c. fresh kale, chopped
1 c. grape tomatoes, cut in half
1 to 2 carrots, peeled and
    chopped

1 cucumber, peeled, quartered
    and sliced
1/4 c. chopped pecans
raspberry vinaigrette or other
    salad dressing to taste

Combine all ingredients in a large bowl; toss to mix. Serve with your favorite salad dressing. Makes 4 to 6 servings.

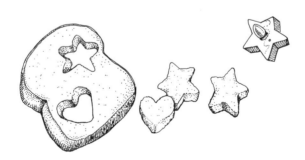

Turn leftover bread into toasty salad croutons. Toss bread cubes with olive oil, garlic powder and dried herbs. Bake on a baking sheet at 400 degrees for 5 to 10 minutes, until toasty and golden.

I'll Be Home for *Christmas* Cookbook

Granny Smith Apple Salad

Karen Permenter
Arnold, MO

*My husband and I make this salad for all our family functions.
We have made it for potlucks at work, too...it is highly
requested! The dressing is simple, yet so delicious.*

2 heads red leaf lettuce, chopped
3 Granny Smith apples, cored
    and thinly sliced
2 stalks celery, diced

3 green onions, diced
8-oz. pkg. Gorgonzola cheese,
    diced

Prepare Candied Walnuts and Apple Cider Vinaigrette ahead of time. To
assemble, combine lettuce, apples, celery, onions and cheese in a large
bowl. Drizzle generously with vinaigrette; top with walnuts. Makes
12 servings.

Candied Walnuts:

2 c. walnut halves

1/2 c. sugar

Place walnuts in a skillet over high heat; add sugar. Cook, stirring
constantly, until sugar caramelizes and walnuts are thoroughly coated.
Spread walnuts on parchment paper to cool.

Apple Cider Vinaigrette:

1/3 c. cider vinegar
2/3 c. canola oil
1/3 c. sugar

1 t. pepper
3 splashes hot pepper sauce

Combine all ingredients in a squirt bottle; shake vigorously.

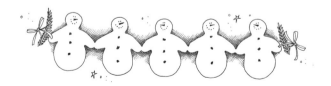

I am in holiday humor!
–William Shakespeare

Seasonal Salads & Sides

Lelia's Famous Cranberry Salad

Julie Wiesen
Houston, TX

My friend's mom from Trenton, Kentucky gave me this recipe 30 years ago and it has turned into a mainstay at my extended family's Thanksgiving and Christmas celebrations. Kids and adults all devour it...we always have to make extra batches!

3-1/2 c. fresh cranberries
1-1/2 c. sugar
8-oz. can crushed pineapple, drained

1 c. chopped pecans
16-oz. pkg. mini marshmallows
1 pt. whipping cream

Grind cranberries in a food processor; transfer to a large bowl. Add remaining ingredients except cream; mix well and set aside. In a deep bowl, with an electric mixer on high speed, beat cream until soft peaks form. Fold whipped cream into cranberry mixture. Cover and refrigerate until chilled. Serves 10.

Grape Salad

Vivian Schweppe
Greensburg, PA

At family gatherings and church functions, this is the first to go!

8-oz. pkg. cream cheese, softened
1/2 c. sugar
1 T. vanilla extract

1 lb. seedless red grapes
1 lb. seedless green grapes
1/3 c. brown sugar, packed
1 c. chopped pecans

In a large bowl, blend together cream cheese, sugar and vanilla. Add grapes; stir to coat well. Spread in a 13"x9" glass baking pan. In another bowl, combine brown sugar and pecans; sprinkle over top. Cover and refrigerate until serving time. Serves 8 to 12.

Cover a table with gift wrap... kids big & little will love it!

Artichoke-Rice Salad

Shirley Howie
Foxboro, MA

The longer this salad chills, the better the flavor! I like to make it a day ahead to allow the flavors to blend overnight. So convenient, too, for gatherings, potlucks or picnics. It's easily doubled as needed.

2 c. chicken broth
1 c. long-cooking rice, uncooked
6-1/2 oz. jar marinated
   artichokes, drained and
   halved
1/4 c. green olives with
   pimentos, halved
1/4 c. green onions, chopped
1/4 c. green pepper, chopped
1/2 c. mayonnaise
1 t. dill weed, or to taste
1/2 t. salt
1/8 t. pepper
Garnish: additional sliced
   green olives

In a saucepan over high heat, bring chicken broth to a boil. Stir in rice; return to a boil. Reduce heat to medium-low; cover and simmer for 20 minutes, or until rice is tender. Transfer rice to a large bowl; cool. Add remaining ingredients except garnish; stir until well combined. Cover and chill thoroughly. At serving time, garnish with additional sliced olives. Serves 4 to 5.

Set up a small tree for the kids...a great way for them to show off favorite ornaments of their very own. If your children are grown, they'll love it even more!

Seasonal
Salads & Sides

Shrimp & Pasta Shell Salad

Carolyn Ballard
Rochester Hills, MI

*Everyone loves this delicious hearty salad. Crabmeat can be
used instead of shrimp, if you like.*

16-oz. pkg. small shell pasta,
    uncooked
6-oz. jar marinated artichoke
    hearts, drained
4-oz. can sliced black olives,
    drained
1/2 c. banana pepper rings,
    drained

1 tomato, sliced
16-oz. pkg. frozen cooked
    shrimp, thawed and chopped
16-oz. pkg. shredded Cheddar
    cheese
Italian salad dressing to taste

Cook pasta according to package directions; drain and rinse in cold
water. In a large bowl, combine pasta and remaining ingredients except
salad dressing. Toss to mix; add dressing to taste. Cover and chill at
least 15 minutes before serving. Serves 8 to 10.

Jo's Favorite Chicken Salad

Emilie Britton
New Bremen, OH

*Everyone loves this chicken salad! It's wonderful served on shredded
lettuce or in pita bread. This recipe is named for my sister Joann.*

1/2 c. mayonnaise
1/4 c. sour cream
3 c. cooked chicken, chopped

1/2 c. seedless green or red
    grapes, halved
3/4 c. toasted chopped pecans

In a serving bowl, combine mayonnaise and sour cream. Stir in chicken,
grapes and pecans; cover and chill. Make 4 to 6 servings.

Sending a Christmas card to a
special friend? Tuck in a packet
of spiced tea...she'll be delighted!

Tangy Broccoli-Mushroom Salad

Michelle McLendon
Indianapolis, IN

This has been a family requirement for almost 30 years! It's tangy, and if there are any leftovers, it just gets tastier after chilling. Be sure to wait until close to serving time to add the dressing, especially if your family likes crunchy sunflower seeds! I usually mix it up to dress each bite of salad, transfer into a serving bowl, and then just put the sunflower seeds on the table for people to add their own.

2 to 3 heads broccoli, cut into
    bite-size flowerets
1 lb. sliced mushrooms

1 white onion, diced
1 c. salted roasted sunflower
    seeds

Make Dressing ahead of time. Shortly before serving time, lightly toss vegetables in a large bowl. Remove dressing from refrigerator and blend well. Pour dressing over vegetables and toss to cover. Sprinkle with sunflower seeds at serving time. Leftovers will keep in the refrigerator for a couple of days, but the dressing will get more tart the longer it stands. Serves 10 to 12.

Dressing:

1 c. oil
1/3 c. sugar
1/3 c. red wine vinegar

1 t. garlic powder
1 t. celery seed
1 t. pepper

Combine all ingredients in a jar with a tight-fitting lid; cover and shake well. Refrigerate for at least one hour.

Baked sweet potatoes are delicious and easy. Pierce several times with a fork and bake until tender, about 45 minutes at 400 degrees.

Seasonal
Salads & Sides

That Good Salad

JoAnn
Gooseberry Patch

*My family loves this salad! It's so easy to make, and all the
ingredients are available year 'round. If you need to feed
a few more more people, just add another head of lettuce.*

2 heads romaine lettuce, torn
2 c. cherry tomatoes
1 c. shredded Swiss cheese
1/2 c. grated Parmesan cheese

8 slices bacon, crisply cooked
    and crumbled
1 c. Caesar salad croutons

Make Dressing ahead of time; chill. In a large serving bowl, combine all
ingredients except croutons; toss to mix well. Shake Dressing again;
drizzle over salad and toss again. Add croutons and serve immediately.
Serves 8 to 10.

Dressing:

3/4 c. canola oil
1/4 c. lemon juice
2 cloves garlic, minced

1/2 t. salt
1/2 t. pepper

Combine all ingredients in a jar with a tight-fitting lid. Cover and shake
well; chill.

Bundle up the kids and take a ride to enjoy all the
holiday lights...the kids can even wear their pajamas!
Wrap up in cozy blankets, sing carols and enjoy a
fun-filled evening making memories together.

I'll Be Home for *Christmas* Cookbook

Cranberry-Spinach Salad

Kelly Nicholson
Gooseberry Patch

Perfect for any holiday meal!

1/4 c. white wine vinegar
1/4 c. cider vinegar
1/2 c. oil
1/4 c. sugar
2 T. toasted sesame seed

1 T. poppy seed
2 t. dried, minced onion
1/4 t. paprika
1 lb. fresh spinach, torn
1 c. sweetened dried cranberries

Prepare Toasted Almonds ahead of time. In a bowl, whisk together all ingredients except spinach and cranberries; cover and chill. Just before serving, combine spinach, cranberries and almonds in a large bowl. Drizzle with dressing; toss to coat well. Serves 8.

Toasted Almonds:

1 T. butter

3/4 c. slivered almonds

Melt butter in a saucepan over medium heat. Add almonds; cook and stir until lightly toasted. Drain almonds on paper towels.

A cheery, painted chalkboard is ideal for counting down the days until Christmas.

Tootsie's Rotini Pasta Salad
Mary Jefferson Rabon
Mobile, AL

My dad first started making pasta salad years ago for our family get-togethers. Now that he's gone and missed so much, I've added a few things and carried on the tradition...it is always requested! Some good additions are small broccoli flowerets, sliced pepperoni, red pepper or pimento, feta cheese and cheese tortellini. But the basic salad is enjoyed even by picky eaters.

2 16-oz. pkgs. rotini pasta,
    uncooked
2 4-oz. cans medium black
    olives, drained and chopped
1 c. shredded Parmesan cheese,
    or more to taste

3/4 c. shredded Cheddar cheese
6 green onions, chopped
3 T. salad seasoning
16-oz. bottle Italian salad
    dressing, or to taste

Cook pasta according to package directions; drain and rinse in cold water. Transfer pasta to a large serving bowl; add remaining ingredients and toss to mix well. Cover and chill. Serves 15 to 20.

Slip a fun photo into a frame...a terrific gift
that's sure to be treasured!

I'll Be Home for *Christmas* Cookbook

Crunchy Pea Salad

Sandy Ann Ward
Anderson, IN

From the ladies of Grandma Nellie's church...this recipe is tried & true!

10-oz. pkg. frozen peas, thawed
1 c. celery with leaves, chopped
1 c. cauliflower, chopped
1/4 c. green onions, chopped
1/2 c. sour cream

1/2 t. spicy mustard
salt and pepper to taste
Optional: crisply cooked
   crumbled bacon

Combine all ingredients in a large bowl; mix well. Cover and chill until serving time. Makes 8 servings.

Show off Christmas photos from years past in a wire card holder. Family & friends will love taking a trip down memory lane with you.

Seasonal
Salads & Sides

Broccoli Slaw with Ramen Noodles

Teresa Verell
Roanoke, VA

My family always enjoys this salad at our New Year's Day brunch.

1 lb. broccoli slaw
1/2 c. onion, chopped
3-oz. pkg. chicken ramen
    noodles with seasoning
    packet

1 c. zesty Italian salad dressing
1/3 c. sugar
1/3 c. peanut oil
3 T. red wine vinegar
1 c. chopped cashews

In a large bowl, combine broccoli slaw and onion. Break up noodles and add to mixture; stir gently and set aside. In a separate bowl, combine seasoning packet and remaining ingredients except cashews; stir until sugar dissolves. Add dressing mixture to slaw mixture; toss well. Cover and refrigerate for 2 hours. Add cashews just before serving. Mix well. Makes 6 servings.

Fill Mason jars with several inches of Epsom salt or sand and drop a votive candle into each. Group them on the front porch or winding up the walkway for a cheery welcome.

Raspberry Carousel Salad

Annette Ceravolo
Birmingham, AL

I've had this recipe for over 25 years and it's still a favorite with family & friends. To save calories, I use sugar-free gelatin and light mayonnaise. Tastes just as great and no one has to know you shaved off a few calories. Shhh!

2 3-oz. pkgs. raspberry
    gelatin mix
4 c. boiling water, divided
1-1/2 c. cranberry juice cocktail
2 c. apples, peeled, cored and
    diced

1/2 c. celery, chopped
1 c. chopped pecans
2 3-oz. pkgs. lemon gelatin mix
8-oz. container frozen whipped
    topping, thawed
1/2 c. mayonnaise

In a bowl, combine raspberry gelatin and 2 cups boiling water. Stir for 2 minutes, or until dissolved. Add cranberry juice; chill for about one hour. Fold in apples, celery and pecans; transfer to a clear glass serving bowl. Cover and chill for 15 to 20 minutes. In another bowl, dissolve lemon gelatin in 2 cups boiling water. Chill for about 45 minutes, until slightly thickened. Fold whipped topping and mayonnaise into lemon gelatin. Carefully spread over raspberry mixture; cover and chill overnight, or until firm. Serves 8 to 10.

For a sparkling, "snowy" centerpiece, nestle votives and tealights on a cake stand sprinkled with rock salt.

Seasonal
Salads & Sides

Aunt Jo's Coconut Fluff

Ramona Wysong
Barlow, KY

My aunt's recipe is great for get-togethers and celebrations.
Easy to make and everyone loves it!

16-oz. container frozen whipped
    topping, thawed
30-oz. can fruit cocktail, drained
2 c. mini marshmallows

1 c. flaked coconut
1/4 c. maraschino cherries,
    chopped
1/4 c. chopped pecans

In a large bowl, mix together whipped topping and fruit cocktail. Fold in
remaining ingredients; spoon into a serving bowl. Cover and refrigerate
for several hours, or overnight for the best taste. Serves 8 to 12.

Pearl's Fruit Salad

Evangeline Boston
Ellenton, FL

My mom used to make this salad at Christmas. It's simple but really
tastes good. She passed away many years ago, yet her recipe is still
made every Christmas. Other fruit can be added as you like.

20-oz. can pineapple chunks,
    drained and juice reserved
11-oz. can mandarin oranges,
    drained and juice reserved

2 ripe bananas, sliced
1 c. mini marshmallows
3.4-oz. pkg. instant lemon
    pudding mix

Combine pineapple and oranges in a large bowl; set aside 3/4 cup
reserved juices. Add bananas and marshmallows; sprinkle with dry
pudding mix. Add reserved juices; stir until well moistened. Cover and
chill until serving time. Makes 8 to 10 servings.

Sprinkle ruby-red pomegranate
seeds on salads for a splash of
holiday color.

Ridiculously Good Scalloped Potatoes

Cindy Kemp
Lake Jackson, TX

This is the most wonderful scalloped potato dish I have ever tasted!
You don't even need to peel the potatoes if they're thin-skinned. While
it is great the first day it is made, the second day is even better...
if there are any leftovers, that is!

2-1/4 lbs. russet potatoes
salt and cracked pepper to taste
14-1/2 oz. can chicken broth
1-1/2 c. whipping cream or
    half-and-half
4 t. garlic, minced

1-1/2 t. dried sage, or
    1/2 t. rubbed sage
2/3 c. shredded Cheddar cheese
1/3 c. shredded Gorgonzola
    cheese

Thinly slice potatoes, using a mandoline if possible; place in a large
bowl. Season with salt and pepper; set aside. In a heavy saucepan over
medium heat, combine broth, whipping cream or half-and-half, garlic
and sage. Simmer for 5 minutes, or until slightly thickened; do not boil.
Add cheeses and stir until melted; remove from heat. Arrange half of
the potatoes in a lightly greased 13"x9" glass baking pan. Pour half of
cream mixture over potatoes; repeat layering. Bake, uncovered, at
375 degrees for one to 1-1/4 hours, until golden and potatoes are
tender. Let stand about 15 minutes before serving. Serves 6 to 8.

Take the family to a pottery painting class...what a fun time
they'll have creating holiday plates and cups to share!

Seasonal
Salads & Sides

Lemony Skillet Broccoli

Barb Bargdill
Gooseberry Patch

*The green color and fresh taste of this broccoli really
brightens a plate of meat and potatoes.*

1 lemon
1 T. olive oil
1 yellow onion, cut into 1-inch
    wedges
2 cloves garlic, pressed
1 t. ground coriander

1/4 t. red pepper flakes
1 bunch broccoli, cut into
    flowerets
2 c. water
salt and pepper to taste

Pare 4 wide strips of zest from lemon. Cut lemon into 4 wedges and set
aside. In a large skillet, heat oil over medium-high heat. Add onion;
cook for about 6 minutes, stirring occasionally, until golden. Add garlic,
coriander and red pepper flakes; cook for 30 seconds. Add broccoli,
lemon zest strips and water; bring to a boil. Reduce heat to medium-
low. Cover and cook until fork-tender, about 8 minutes. Season with
salt and pepper; serve with reserved lemon wedges. Serves 4.

Freshly grated citrus zest adds so much flavor to recipes,
and it's easy to keep on hand. Whenever you use an orange,
lemon or lime, just grate the peel first. Keep it frozen in an
airtight container for up to 2 months.

Sour Cream Zucchini Casserole

Debbie Douma
Pensacola, FL

In "another life" I was a military officer's wife. During deployments, wives unable to travel to their hometowns would get together to celebrate holidays. This dish was brought to a Thanksgiving potluck over 25 years ago, and it became a family favorite. I also serve it as a meatless main dish.

3 to 4 zucchini, chopped
1/2 c. onion, chopped
6 T. butter, divided
6-oz. pkg. herb-flavored
    stuffing mix

1-1/2 c. water
8-oz. container sour cream

Combine zucchini, onion and 2 tablespoons butter in a microwave-safe dish. Cover and microwave on high for 10 minutes, stirring occasionally. Meanwhile, prepare stuffing mix with water and remaining butter, as directed on package. Add sour cream and half of stuffing to zucchini mixture; mix well and transfer to a lightly greased 13"x9" baking pan. Sprinkle remaining stuffing mix on top. Bake, uncovered, at 350 degrees for 35 to 40 minutes. Makes 6 to 8 servings.

At last the dinner was all done, the cloth was cleaned, the hearth swept and the fire made up. A Merry Christmas to us all, my dears. God bless us! Which all the family re-echoed. God bless us every one.

–Charles Dickens

Seasonal
Salads & Sides

Updated Green Bean Casserole

Tina Wright
Atlanta, GA

My husband can't stand mushroom soup, but he loves those crispy onions, so I was happy when I found this recipe. We love it!

16-oz. pkg. frozen French-cut
   green beans
2 T. butter
1/4 c. all-purpose flour

1 c. chicken broth
1 c. whole milk
1 c. canned French fried onions
1 T. dried, minced onion

Place beans in a microwave-safe 2-quart casserole dish; cover and microwave for 10 minutes. Meanwhile, melt butter in a saucepan over medium heat. Sprinkle with flour; cook and stir for one minute, or until lightly golden. Add broth; cook, whisking constantly, until thickened and smooth. Whisk in milk; cook until thickened. Stir in all the onions. Spoon over beans in dish. Bake, uncovered, at 350 degrees for 30 minutes. Serves 8 to 10.

Roasted Brussels Sprouts & Hazelnuts

Gail Blain
Grand Island, NE

This side dish is easy enough for weeknights, yet good enough for company!

3 T. butter
1-1/2 lbs. Brussels sprouts,
   trimmed and quartered
1/3 c. chopped hazelnuts

1/2 t. salt
1 t. pepper
3 to 4 T. water

Melt butter in a heavy saucepan over medium heat. Cook and stir for 3 minutes, or until browned; remove from heat. Spread Brussels sprouts and hazelnuts on a rimmed baking sheet. Drizzle with butter; season with salt and pepper. Place pan on rack in lower third of oven. Bake at 450 degrees for 14 to 16 minutes, sprinkling with water after 8 minutes, until sprouts are tender and lightly golden. Serves 6.

I'll Be Home for *Christmas* Cookbook

Eleanor's Spinach Gratin

Eleanor Dionne
Beverly, MA

This is a favorite for us at the winter holidays.

1/4 c. butter
4 c. yellow onions, chopped
1/4 c. all-purpose flour
1/4 t. nutmeg
1 c. whipping cream
2 c. whole milk
4 12-oz. pkgs. frozen chopped
   spinach, thawed

1 c. shredded Parmesan cheese,
   divided
1 T. kosher salt
1/2 t. pepper
1/2 c. shredded Gruyère
   cheese

Melt butter in a heavy skillet over medium heat. Add onions and sauté until translucent, about 5 minutes. Sprinkle with flour and nutmeg; cook and stir for 2 more minutes. Add cream and milk; cook, stirring occasionally, until thickened. Squeeze as much liquid as possible from spinach; add spinach to sauce in skillet. Add 1/2 cup Parmesan cheese; mix well. Season with salt and pepper. Transfer to a lightly greased 13"x9" baking pan; sprinkle with Gruyère cheese and remaining Parmesan cheese. Bake at 425 degrees for 20 minutes, or until hot and bubbly. Serve immediately. Serves 8 to 10.

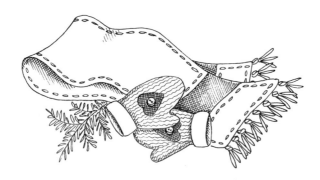

Lots of family members to buy for? Choose a single item like woolly knitted scarves or cozy winter slippers to buy for everyone, in different colors and textures.

Seasonal Salads & Sides

Caroline's Whipped Butternut Squash

Lisa Engwell
Bellevue, NE

I adapted this easy recipe from a recipe I found. My daughter Caroline loves it so much that I named the recipe after her! It's wonderful any time of the year. For holidays it's a perfect side dish.

2-1/2 lb. butternut squash,
    peeled and cubed
3 c. water
3/4 t. salt, divided

2 T. butter
1/4 c. light or dark brown sugar,
    packed
1/8 to 1/4 t. nutmeg

In a large saucepan over medium-high heat, combine squash, water and 1/2 teaspoon salt. Bring to a boil; reduce heat to medium. Cover and simmer for 20 minutes, or until squash is fork-tender. Drain; transfer to a bowl. Add butter, brown sugar, nutmeg and remaining salt. Beat with an electric mixer on medium speed until smooth. Makes 6 servings.

Place newly arrived Christmas cards in a vintage napkin holder, then take a moment every evening to share happy holiday greetings from friends & neighbors over dinner!

Sweet Potato Crisp

Becky Gentrup
Shakopee, MN

This is a little twist on a holiday favorite. I'd been making my sweet potato casserole the same way for years, and my son suggested that I change it up by adding an apple crisp-type topping. I was skeptical, but gave it a try...it was delicious!

4-1/2 c. sweet potatoes, peeled, cubed, cooked and mashed
3/4 c. sugar
3/8 c. milk

1/2 c. butter, melted
1-1/2 t. vanilla extract
2 eggs, beaten

In a large saucepan, cover sweet potatoes with water; bring to a boil over high heat. Cook until fork-tender; drain. Add potatoes to a large bowl; mash well. Add remaining ingredients; mix well. Spoon potato mixture into a greased 2-quart casserole dish. Spoon Topping over casserole. Bake, uncovered, at 375 degrees for about 30 minutes, until crisp and golden. Serves 10 to 12.

Topping:

1-1/2 c. all-purpose flour
3/4 c. sugar
3/4 c. light brown sugar, packed

1 c. old-fashioned oats, uncooked
1/2 t. salt
1 c. chilled butter, diced

In a large bowl, mix all ingredients except butter. Add butter; beat with an electric mixer on medium speed until well mixed.

Beeswax candles have such a sweet fragrance...wrap up a bundle and tie with a length of wide rick rack for a gift from the heart. Or choose bayberry candles, said to bring good luck.

Seasonal
Salads & Sides

Hashbrown Potato Bake

Lisa Seckora
Chippewa Falls, WI

This is an easy recipe to make ahead and bake later. I grew up in Saint Anthony, Idaho and potatoes were a favorite staple! Now my family & friends all love this tasty casserole dish.

1 c. milk
2/3 c. cream cheese, plain or
   with chives, softened
4 t. mustard
1/2 t. garlic salt
1/4 t. pepper

32-oz. pkg. frozen diced
   hashbrowns, thawed
6 slices bacon, crisply cooked
   and crumbled, or 1/4 c. bacon
   bits

In a large saucepan over low heat, combine all ingredients except hashbrowns and bacon. Cook and stir until smooth and melted. Remove from heat; add hashbrowns and mix gently. Transfer to a greased 2-quart casserole dish; sprinkle with bacon. Cover and chill up to 24 hours, or bake right away. Bake, covered, at 350 degrees for 45 to 60 minutes, until hot and bubbly. Makes 6 to 8 servings.

When purchasing a fresh-cut Christmas tree, ask about trimmed-off branches. They're often available at little or no cost and are so handy for adding seasonal color and fresh pine scent to your home.

Nutty Wild Rice

Melody Taynor
Everett, WA

My in-laws in Minnesota like to send us a wild rice gift pack every year for the holidays. This is one of the tastiest recipes I've found to use it with. You can add some cooked, cubed turkey or chicken for a delicious main dish.

2 t. olive oil	1-1/2 c. water
1/2 c. onion, finely chopped	3/4 t. salt
2 cloves garlic, minced	1/2 t. pepper
2 stalks celery, diced	1/4 t. dried thyme
1 carrot, peeled and chopped	1/4 c. pecans or walnuts,
1 c. wild rice, uncooked	coarsely chopped
1-1/2 c. chicken broth	1/4 c. dried cranberries

Heat oil in a saucepan over medium heat; add onion and garlic. Cook until onion is tender, about 6 minutes. Add celery and carrot. Cook, stirring often, until carrot is tender, about 5 minutes. Stir in rice, broth, water and seasonings; bring to a boil. Reduce heat to medium-low. Cover and simmer for about one hour, checking after 45 minutes, until rice is tender. Meanwhile, add nuts to a dry skillet over low heat. Cook and stir until toasted, about 5 minutes. Just before serving, stir nuts and cranberries into rice mixture. Makes 4 servings.

Be sure to share family stories at Christmastime...they're super conversation starters. How about the time Grandma set out cookies to cool and Skippy the dog ate them, or the year a big snowstorm led to a houseful of extra Christmas guests? It's such fun to share stories like these!

Seasonal
Salads & Sides

Mushroom Dressing

Marta Norton
Redlands, CA

I mean, really? What goes better with turkey than this dressing!

28 slices white bread
1 c. butter
8-oz. pkg. sliced mushrooms
3/4 c. onion, chopped
Optional: 1/2 c. celery, chopped

2 t. poultry seasoning
1 t. dried sage
1 t. salt
1 t. pepper
1/2 to 1 c. chicken broth

Place bread slices on baking sheets. Bake at 325 degrees for about 25 minutes, until toasted. Cut into 1/2-inch cubes; set aside. Melt butter in a skillet over medium heat. Cook mushrooms, onion and celery, if using, until onion is translucent. Meanwhile, combine bread cubes and seasonings in a large bowl. Add mushroom mixture and enough broth to moisten as desired. Spoon loosely into a buttered 3-quart casserole dish. Bake, uncovered, at 350 degrees for 20 to 30 minutes, to desired crispness. Serves 10 to 12.

Festive Fruit Relish

Lisa Cunningham
Boothbay, ME

No holiday in our home would be complete without this delicious relish! It's wonderful with chicken and turkey recipes, freezes well and is a perfect side dish for any family get-together.

3 c. fresh or frozen cranberries
2 apples, quartered and cored

1 orange, peeled and quartered
1 c. sugar

Grind all fruits in a food processor. Transfer to a bowl; stir in sugar. Cover and refrigerate at least 4 hours before serving. This keeps well up to one week in the refrigerator. Makes 8 to 10 servings.

A flavorful drizzle for steamed veggies...simmer 1/2 cup balsamic vinegar until thickened, stirring often.

Lisa's Corn Soufflé

Julie Harris
Fleetwood, PA

My mom always made sure that this side dish found its way into the Thanksgiving and Christmas spreads while I was growing up. Now that I've grown, married and moved away from home, I remember all of my childhood family gathered around the table whenever I make this dish. It's wonderful served on its own or drizzled with maple syrup.

8-1/2 oz. pkg. corn muffin mix
15-1/4 oz. can corn
14-3/4 oz. can creamed corn
8-oz. container sour cream

2 eggs, beaten
1/2 c. butter, melted
Optional: maple syrup

In a bowl, combine dry muffin mix and remaining ingredients except syrup; mix well. Spoon into a greased 13"x9" baking pan. Cover and bake at 350 degrees for one to 1-1/2 hours, until golden and a toothpick inserted in the center comes out clean. Serve topped with maple syrup, if desired. Makes 8 servings.

Christmas may be a day of feasting, or of prayer,
but always it will be a day of remembrance...
a day in which we think of everything
we have ever loved.

–Augusta E. Rundel

Seasonal
Salads & Sides

Special Spinach Casserole

Joyceann Dreibelbis
Wooster, OH

A delicious side dish for a holiday dinner.
I usually have to double the recipe...it's that good!

10-oz. pkg. chopped spinach,
   thawed and drained
2 eggs, hard-boiled, peeled
   and chopped
1/2 lb. bacon, crisply cooked
   and crumbled

1/2 lb. sliced mushrooms
3/4 c. onion, chopped
8-oz. container sour cream
2/3 c. shredded Cheddar
   cheese

Combine spinach and eggs in an ungreased shallow 9"x9" baking pan;
toss together. Sprinkle with bacon; layer with mushrooms and onion. In
a bowl, mix together sour cream and cheese; spread over top. Bake,
uncovered, at 350 degrees for 30 to 35 minutes, until golden. Serves 6.

Parmesan Potato Stacks

Audrey Lett
Newark, DE

Elegant and easy...delicious with baked ham or chicken.

3 T. butter, melted
2 T. grated Parmesan cheese
1 t. garlic powder
1 t. dried thyme

salt and pepper to taste
8 to 10 Yukon Gold potatoes,
   peeled and very thinly sliced

In a large bowl, combine all ingredients except potatoes; mix well.
Add potato slices and turn gently to coat well. Stack potato slices in
12 well-buttered muffin cups, filling cups to the top. Bake at 375 degrees
for 55 minutes to one hour, until potatoes are tender and golden.
Serves 4 to 6.

If you bought a big bag of
potatoes for the holidays, tuck
an apple into the bag...it will
keep them from sprouting.

Creamy Holiday Carrots

Vickie White
Tooele, UT

A friend of mine shared this recipe. It is served at all of their holiday parties. I've tweaked it a little to make it my own. It is so creamy, sweet and delicious. A great side dish for holiday meals...definitely a crowd favorite.

2 lbs. carrots, peeled and thinly sliced	1/2 c. whipping cream
1/4 c. butter	1/4 c. sugar
1 t. all-purpose flour	1/8 t. nutmeg
	1/8 t. salt

In a saucepan, cover carrots with water. Cook over high heat until carrots are tender-crisp; drain and set aside in a bowl. Melt butter in same saucepan over medium heat; sprinkle with flour. Cook until flour is dissolved and turns golden. Add remaining ingredients; cook and stir until sugar is dissolved and sauce is thickened. Return carrots to pan. Cook, stirring gently, until heated through and sauce coats the carrots. Makes 6 to 8 servings.

Cranberry Beets

Annette Ceravolo
Birmingham, AL

If you like beets, you'll love these! This is a different and delicious way to serve them.

2 13-1/4 oz. cans sliced beets, drained	1/4 c. frozen orange juice concentrate
15-oz. can whole-berry cranberry sauce	

Combine all ingredients in a large saucepan. Cook and stir over low heat until heated through. Serve with a slotted spoon. Makes 8 servings.

Make notes all year 'round...at Christmastime, you'll know just what to get everyone!

Seasonal
Salads & Sides

Bell Candied Sweet Potatoes

Sharon Buxton
Warsaw, OH

*This simple yet delicious sweet potato dish was always a part
of our family holiday gatherings, from my grandmother's,
to my mother's, to my own table.*

6 sweet potatoes
1 t. salt
1/4 c. butter

1 c. brown sugar, packed
1/4 c. water

In a stockpot, cover potatoes in skins with water. Cook over high heat
until soft but not mushy, about 20 minutes. Drain and cool; remove
skins and cut lengthwise. Arrange potato halves in a buttered
13"x9" baking pan; sprinkle with salt. In a saucepan over medium heat,
melt butter with brown sugar; add water. Bring to a boil; pour over
potatoes. Bake, uncovered, at 350 degrees for 30 to 45 minutes, until
potatoes are tender and liquid is thickened. Makes 8 to 10 servings.

Curried Acorn Squash

Nola Coons
Gooseberry Patch

This sweet & savory squash is delicious and just a little different.

1 acorn squash, cut into wedges
    and seeds removed
1 T. water

1/4 c. apricot preserves
1/2 t. curry powder
salt and pepper to taste

Place squash wedges in a 13"x9" baking pan; add water to pan. Bake,
uncovered, at 375 degrees for 30 minutes. Meanwhile, combine
remaining ingredients. Spoon mixture over squash and bake,
uncovered, 10 minutes more, or until tender. Serves 4 to 6.

Pennsylvania Dutch Filling

Bethanna Kortie
Greer, SC

My husband craves this dressing almost as much as the turkey at Thanksgiving and Christmas! I save the ends of my bread in the freezer all year long to make this recipe. Serve with roast turkey and plenty of gravy.

2 sliced loaves white bread
1 c. butter
1-1/2 onions, diced
6 stalks celery, diced
2 t. poultry seasoning
2 t. garlic salt
2 t. pepper
6 eggs, beaten
Optional: chicken broth or milk

Lay out bread slices on the countertop overnight to dry out slightly. Tear bread into bite-size pieces; divide between 2 large bowls and set aside. Melt butter in a skillet over medium heat; add onions, celery and seasonings. Sauté until onions are translucent; cool to room temperature. Divide eggs between bowls; divide onion mixture between bowls. Mix with your hands until bread is slightly moistened. For a moister filling, stir in milk or broth as desired. Butter two 20-inch pieces of aluminum foil. Form filling into 2 loaves; place one loaf on each piece of foil. Fold ends of foil over the loaves and seal. Bake at 350 degrees for one hour. Remove foil; slice filling to serve. Makes 10 servings.

For a new spin on the traditional Advent calendar, tuck notes, wrapped candies and games into numbered stockings...a great way to count down the days until Santa's visit!

Seasonal
Salads & Sides

Green Rice

Regina Wickline
Pebble Beach, CA

It doesn't take long at all to make this special rice. Add some
chopped pimentos for a Christmasy touch.

1 c. green onions, thinly sliced
1/4 c. butter
3 c. chicken broth
1-1/3 c. long-cooking rice,
    uncooked

1/2 c. green pepper, diced
1/2 c. fresh parsley, minced
1/4 t. pepper
Optional: 1/2 c. shredded
    Cheddar cheese

In a skillet over medium heat, sauté onions in butter until tender. Stir in broth, rice, green pepper, parsley and pepper. Bring to a boil; remove from heat. Spoon into a greased 2-quart casserole dish. Cover and bake at 350 degrees for 25 minutes, or until rice is tender. Top with cheese, if desired. Bake an additional 3 minutes, or until cheese melts. Makes 4 servings.

Green Beans with a Twist

Connie Ramsey
Pontotoc, MS

My family loves these green beans! I often take them to potlucks too...
I am almost always asked for the recipe.

4 slices bacon, chopped
2 lbs. fresh green beans, trimmed
2 T. butter

1-oz. pkg. ranch salad dressing
    mix

In a Dutch oven over medium heat, sauté bacon until crisp. Using a slotted spoon, remove bacon to paper towels to drain. Add beans and butter to drippings in skillet; sauté for about 10 minutes. Reduce heat to medium-low; simmer until beans reach desired tenderness. Sprinkle with dressing mix; toss to coat. Just before serving, sprinkle with crisp bacon. Makes 6 to 8 servings.

Need a tiny funnel for filling those holiday salt shakers? Cut a corner piece from an envelope, then snip away the tip.

Lucille's Bean Casserole

Sherrie Burkett
Jefferson City, TN

This recipe was my Grandma Lucy's. I remember when I was a little girl going to my Grandma's for the holidays, she would make this and I loved it. I would say to her, "I'm going to make this when I'm a mom." Now I am a grandmother and have passed down the recipe to my daughter.

6 slices bacon, diced
3/4 c. onion, thinly sliced
28-oz. can pork & beans
15-1/2 oz. can kidney beans

14-1/2 oz. can lima beans
1/2 c. catsup
1/2 c. brown sugar, packed
2 t. vinegar

Cook bacon in a skillet over medium heat until crisp; set aside bacon on paper towels to drain. Add onion to drippings; sauté until tender. Meanwhile, in a greased 2-quart casserole dish, combine undrained pork & beans, kidney beans and lima beans. Add bacon, onion and remaining ingredients to bean mixture; stir gently. Bake, uncovered, at 325 degrees for 60 to 90 minutes, until hot and bubbly. May also use a 3-quart slow cooker; cover and cook on low setting for 4 to 5 hours. Makes 6 servings.

Transform a simple pillar candle into a holiday welcome with colorful ball-headed straight pins. Simply push the pins in place to create a snowflake pattern.

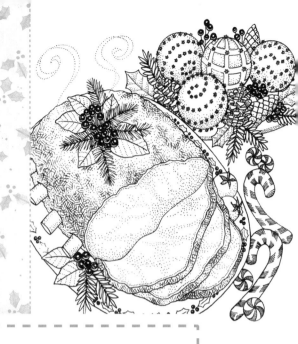

Gathering
with
Family &
Friends

Christmas Shepherd's Pie

Marla Kinnersley
Surprise, AZ

This is comfort food at its finest! It's so easy to make...perfect to serve in the holiday season because of the red and green colors. We really like it on Christmas Eve with a side salad. I hope your family enjoys it as much as we do!

1 lb. ground beef
3/4 c. yellow onion, diced
1 t. garlic powder
10-1/2 oz. can tomato soup
2 14-1/2 oz. cans green
    beans, drained

8-oz. pkg. instant mashed
    potato flakes
8-oz. pkg. shredded Cheddar
    cheese

In a skillet over medium heat, cook beef with onion until beef is no longer pink; drain. Stir in garlic powder, tomato soup and green beans. Spoon beef mixture into a lightly greased 13"x9" baking pan. Prepare potato flakes according to package directions; spread over beef mixture. Top with cheese. Bake, uncovered, at 350 degrees for 30 minutes. Let stand for 10 minutes before serving. Makes 8 servings.

Go ahead and unpack the Christmas tableware early
in December. Even the simplest meal is special
when served on holly-trimmed plates!

Cheesy Chicken-Broccoli Casserole

Vickie
Gooseberry Patch

This tasty dish is simple to toss together...perfect for the busy days leading up to Christmas! Sometimes I'll use fresh broccoli instead of frozen. Cut into spears or flowerets and steam until tender-crisp.

6-oz. pkg. chicken-flavored stuffing mix
16-oz. pkg. frozen broccoli flowerets, thawed and drained
1-1/2 lbs. boneless, skinless chicken breasts, cubed

10-3/4 oz. can cream of chicken soup
8-oz. pkg. pasteurized process cheese, cubed

Prepare stuffing as directed on package; set aside. Arrange broccoli in a lightly greased 13"x9" baking pan; top with chicken. Spoon soup over all; top with cheese. Spoon stuffing over cheese. Bake, uncovered, at 400 degrees for 40 minutes, or until bubbly and chicken is cooked through. Serves 4 to 6.

Make grown-ups feel like kids again! Stuff stockings with penny candy, comic books, card games and other childhood delights. Hang from the backs of dining room chairs with tasseled cords.

Chicken & Zucchini Stew

Karen Crooks
Ankeny, IA

I love this simple recipe that's easy yet impressive enough for guests. This is not really a stew...it is served on a platter, with the pan juices ladled over! I received this delicious recipe many years ago from a co-worker who enjoyed cooking French-inspired recipes.

1-1/2 t. salt, divided	2 zucchini, cut into one-inch
1/4 t. pepper	slices
1/2 t. paprika	1 stalk celery, cut into one-inch
3-1/2 lb. broiler-fryer chicken,	slices
or favorite chicken pieces	1/2 c. white wine or chicken
2 T. oil	broth
1 c. chicken broth	3 T. all-purpose flour
3 redskin potatoes, peeled	1/4 c. cold water
and quartered	Optional: chopped fresh parsley

Combine one teaspoon salt, pepper and paprika in a cup; rub into chicken pieces. Heat oil in a Dutch oven over medium-high heat; brown chicken on all sides. Add broth to pan; bring to a boil. Add potatoes, zucchini, celery and remaining salt. Cover and simmer over medium heat for 15 to 20 minutes, until vegetables are tender and chicken juices run clear when pierced. Add wine or broth to pan; remove chicken and vegetables to a warm platter. Combine flour and water in a cup; blend mixture into pan juices with a whisk. Cook and stir until thickened. Spoon pan juices over chicken and vegetables on platter; garnish as desired. Makes 4 to 6 servings.

Wide-rimmed soup plates are perfect for serving saucy pasta dishes and hearty stews. There's even room to balance a muffin or roll on the edge.

Gathering with Family & Friends

Beef Supper in a Skillet

Rita Frye
King, NC

This isn't a Christmas recipe as such, but I do fix it often during the hectic holidays when time for a sit-down dinner is a luxury. It comes together in less than 30 minutes, is warm and hearty, and a family favorite! I set the skillet on a trivet right on the table, and serve with a dark green leafy salad and cinnamon applesauce. My family always squirts catsup on their portions.

8-oz. pkg. elbow macaroni, uncooked
1 lb. ground beef
4 to 5 slices bacon
10-1/2 oz. can tomato soup
8-oz. pkg. shredded sharp Cheddar cheese
Optional: catsup

Cook macaroni according to package directions; drain well. Meanwhile, brown beef in a large skillet; drain. Place bacon on a microwave-safe dish between several paper towels; microwave on high for 4 to 5 minutes. Stir soup and crumbled or chopped bacon into beef; add cooked macaroni and stir well. Spread cheese on top. Cover skillet and let stand until cheese melts, or put skillet under the broiler for a few minutes. Serve with catsup on the side, if desired. Serves 6.

Turn a white cotton tablecloth into a family memento. Using a permanent marker, ask each family member to sign their name and date it. Younger children can trace around their hands. Sure to be treasured in years to come!

I'll Be Home for *Christmas* Cookbook

Sandy's Chicken Lasagna

Sandy Coffey
Cincinnati, OH

This yummy, super-cheesy recipe compares very favorably to traditional lasagna. It's great for holiday nights when everyone is busy with school concerts, shopping and decorating. Serve with garlic bread and a simple dessert for a wonderful meal.

16-oz. pkg. lasagna noodles, uncooked
3 c. cooked chicken, cubed
10-3/4 oz. can cream of mushroom soup
10-3/4 oz. cream of chicken soup
8-oz. container sour cream

1 c. onion, chopped
2 to 3 t. garlic salt
16-oz. pkg. shredded mozzarella cheese, divided
16-oz. pkg. shredded Cheddar cheese, divided

Cook lasagna noodles according to package directions; drain. Meanwhile, in a bowl, combine chicken, soups, sour cream, onion and garlic salt; mix well. In a greased deep 13"x9" baking pan, layer 1/3 each of the noodles, chicken mixture and cheeses. Repeat layering twice, ending with cheeses on top. Bake, uncovered, at 350 degrees for 40 to 50 minutes, until hot and bubbly. Serves 8 to 10.

Host a tree-trimming party. Invite all the cousins, aunts and uncles for a merry time hanging ornaments and twining garland. Afterwards, share holiday plans over a simple supper. Such fun!

Gathering with Family & Friends

Chicken Enchiladas

Denise Burks
Ore City, TX

Every Christmas when all my family are home, they ask me to make a Mexican dinner. That's my cue to make these special chicken enchiladas.

6 chicken breasts
12 8-inch flour tortillas
1 onion, chopped
1/4 c. jalapeño peppers,
   chopped

2 10-3/4 oz. cans cream of
   chicken soup
8-oz. container sour cream
16-oz. pkg. jalapeño pasteurized
   process cheese, diced

In a stockpot, cover chicken breasts with water. Bring to a boil over high heat; reduce heat to medium-low. Simmer until chicken juices run clear when pierced. Remove chicken to a platter; cool. Cut chicken into cubes, discarding skin and bones. Fill tortillas with chicken, onion and peppers; do not overfill. Roll up tortillas and place in a greased deep 13"x9" baking pan. In a bowl, stir together soup, sour cream and cheese; spread over enchiladas. Bake, uncovered, at 350 degrees for about 45 minutes, until bubbly and heated through. Serves 6, 2 enchiladas each.

Stack several cookies and wrap in plastic wrap. Tie with curling ribbon and tuck in a sprig of holly for a tasty take-home treat to set on each guest's dinner plate.

Grandma's Holiday Beef Brisket

Melanie Springer
Canton, OH

My mom used to make this delicious brisket for many holiday meals. I have continued the tradition and now my sons and daughters-in-law are making it too! It's a great time-saver since the brisket can be baked well ahead of time and refrigerated or frozen.

5 to 7-lb. beef brisket
seasoned salt, pepper and
   paprika to taste
1 to 2 T. olive oil
2 onions, sliced
5 to 7 cloves garlic, chopped
8-oz. pkg. sliced mushrooms

5 carrots, peeled and cut
   into chunks
3 bay leaves
12-oz. bottle chili sauce
1/2 c. brown sugar, packed
1/2 c. red wine or beef broth
1/2 c. water

Sprinkle brisket with seasonings on both sides; place in a roaster and set aside. Heat oil in a skillet over medium heat; add onions and sauté until golden. Add garlic; sauté 3 more minutes. Spread onion mixture over and under brisket. Arrange mushrooms and carrots around brisket; place bay leaves on brisket. Mix remaining ingredients in a bowl; spoon over all. Cover and bake at 325 degrees for 3-1/2 to 4 hours. Allow to cool, discarding bay leaves. Slice brisket and serve with sauce and vegetables from pan. May also wrap and refrigerate or freeze; package brisket and sauce separately. To serve, thaw in refrigerator; skim fat from brisket and and reheat with sauce. Serves 8 to 12.

A sweet placecard friends can take home. Write each friend's name on a vintage Christmas postcard, then clip onto the side of a plate.

Gathering with
Family & Friends

Cranberry Chicken

Bootsie Dominick
Sandy Springs, GA

This is an easy and delicious dish. I love to make it for my family and company at Christmastime. The ruby-red color looks so pretty on holiday china.

4 to 6 boneless, skinless
  chicken breasts
15-oz. can whole-berry
  cranberry sauce

8-oz. bottle red Russian
  salad dressing
1-oz. pkg. onion soup mix
cooked rice

Arrange chicken breasts in a greased 13"x9" baking pan; set aside. Combine remaining ingredients except rice in a bowl; mix well and spoon over chicken. Cover with aluminum foil. Bake at 350 degrees for 30 minutes. Uncover and bake another 20 minutes, or until chicken juices run clear. Serve chicken and sauce over cooked rice. Makes 4 to 6 servings.

Raspberry Pork Chops

Carolyn Deckard
Bedford, IN

This is such a great easy meal to fix. When we have guests, it's easy to double it. Serve with your favorite vegetables.

4 5-oz. boneless pork loin chops
1 T. canola oil
1/4 c. cider vinegar

1/4 c. seedless raspberry jam
1 T. mustard

In a skillet over medium heat, brown pork chops in oil on both sides. Stir in vinegar, jam and mustard; reduce heat to medium-low. Cover and simmer for 10 to 15 minutes, until juices run clear. Remove pork chops to a plate; keep warm. Turn heat to high; cook sauce in pan until reduced by half, stirring occasionally. Spoon sauce over pork chops. Makes 4 servings.

My idea of Christmas, whether old-fashioned or modern, is very simple: loving others.

–Bob Hope

Baked Macaroni My Way

Thomas Hiegel
Union City, OH

I have been cooking for a long time and this deluxe mac & cheese is one of my favorite recipes. I hope you will enjoy it too!

8-oz. pkg. elbow macaroni, uncooked
3 c. chicken broth
4 T. butter, sliced and divided
1/2 c. green pepper, chopped
1/4 c. sweet onion, chopped
1/4 c. celery, finely chopped
1/2 c. sliced mushrooms
1/2 c. sliced green olives with pimentos
1-1/2 c. cooked ham, cubed
1 c. shredded sharp Cheddar cheese
10-1/2 oz. can tomato soup
3 slices bacon

Cook macaroni in broth with one tablespoon butter, according to package directions; drain. Meanwhile, sauté green pepper, onion and celery in remaining butter for about 5 minutes, until soft. Combine cooked macaroni, pepper mixture and remaining ingredients except bacon. Mix well; transfer to a greased 2-quart casserole dish. Arrange bacon slices on top. Bake, uncovered, at 400 degrees for 20 minutes, or until bubbly and bacon is crisp. Makes 6 servings.

Share the joy! Call a local college and invite an out-of-town student to dinner who won't be going home over the long holidays. Or perhaps your church can suggest an older person who is on her own. The more, the merrier!

Gathering with Family & Friends

Easy Ravioli Lasagna with Spinach

Lori Rosenberg
Cleveland, OH

The perfect quick & easy holiday meal for the busy holiday season! Served with a tossed salad and garlic bread, this is a perfect meal for a winter night.

1-1/4 c. marinara sauce, divided
1-1/2 T. Italian salad dressing
  mix, divided
20-oz. pkg. refrigerated cheese
  ravioli, uncooked and divided
10-oz. pkg. frozen chopped
  spinach, thawed and
  squeezed dry

8-oz. pkg. shredded mozzarella
  cheese, divided
1/4 c. grated Parmesan
  cheese

Spread 1/4 cup marinara sauce over the bottom of a lightly greased 8"x8" baking pan. Sprinkle with 1/2 tablepoon dressing mix; arrange half of ravioli over sauce. Spread half of remaining sauce over ravioli; sprinkle with another 1/2 tablespoon dressing mix. Top with all of spinach and half of mozzarella cheese. Repeat with remaining ravioli, sauce, dressing mix and mozzarella cheese. Sprinkle Parmesan cheese on top . Cover with aluminum foil. Bake at 375 degrees for 30 minutes. Remove foil; bake about 10 minutes longer, until hot and bubbly. Let cool for about 5 minutes; slice and serve. Makes 8 servings.

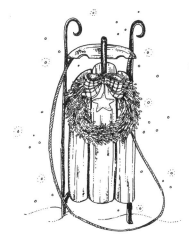

Old-fashioned favorites like a pair of ice skates or a vintage sled by the front door are a sweet welcome for friends. Tie on evergreen boughs, pine cones and red berry sprigs for cheery color.

Easy-Peasy Fancy Ziti

Kelly Craven
Sugar Hill, GA

Any time we have guests over for dinner, or if there is a family from church in need of a meal, I toss this together. It's a meal that everyone will eat, even the pickiest of eaters. Add a loaf of garlic bread and a salad tossed with Italian dressing...you will feel like you are at a fancy Italian restaurant! The best part is, you can make it your own with ingredients that are your favorites.

16-oz. pkg. ziti, rotini or penne
    pasta, uncooked
14-oz. pkg. frozen mini
    meatballs
2 24-oz. jars marinara sauce,
    divided

16-oz. container ricotta cheese
Optional: garlic salt to taste
8-oz. pkg. shredded mozzarella
    cheese

Cook pasta according to package directions; drain. Meanwhile, add meatballs to a microwave-safe bowl; microwave on high for 3 minutes. Remove from microwave; cut meatballs into halves or thirds. Spread some of the sauce over the bottom of a lightly greased 13"x9" glass baking pan. Add cooked pasta and meatballs to pan. Add ricotta cheese by spoonfuls over pasta and meatballs. If needed, smooth out the cheese over the dish. Sprinkle with garlic salt, if desired. Spoon remaining sauce over top; top with mozzarella cheese. Bake, uncovered, at 350 degrees for 25 to 30 minutes, until bubbly and cheese is golden. Serves 6 to 8.

A magnetic knife holder is a handy spot to keep track
of holiday reminders. Attach notes with magnets
from the craft store that have been spruced
up with hot-glued buttons.

Kielbasa & Potato Bake

Jackie Flood
Geneseo, NY

My family just loves this dish! This is a tasty recipe you can play around with, using different kinds of ingredients.

1 lb. Kielbasa sausage, cut
    into chunks
4 potatoes, peeled and cut
    into chunks
1 onion, sliced
1 green pepper, sliced

1 c. dry white wine or
    chicken broth
1/3 c. honey mustard or spicy
    brown mustard
3 T. brown sugar, packed

Combine sausage, potatoes, onion and green pepper in a lightly greased shallow 13"x9" baking pan; set aside. In a small bowl, combine remaining ingredients. Drizzle over sausage mixture and toss to coat. Bake, uncovered, at 400 degrees for 55 minutes, or until potatoes are tender, stirring occasionally. Serves 6.

A place card that doubles as a tree ornament!
Paint a wooden holiday cut-out and add the recipient's
name. Look for fun shapes like angels, mittens and
stars at craft stores.

I'll Be Home for
Christmas
Cookbook

Beef Eye Roast for Sandwiches
Kristie Bouldin
Trinity, NC

This recipe is so delicious, we fell in love with it many years ago. It's so easy to do...great for get-togethers and parties any time!

3 to 4-lb. beef eye roast
2 T. all-purpose flour
2 T. shortening
1/2 c. pineapple juice
1.05-oz. pkg. Italian salad
    dressing mix
1 T. dried, minced onion

1 T. lemon juice
1 T. Worcestershire sauce
2 T. salt
1/8 t. pepper
8 to 10 sandwich buns, split
Optional: coleslaw

Sprinkle roast lightly all over with flour; set aside. In a large Dutch oven with a lid, melt shortening over medium-high heat. Add roast; brown on all sides. In a bowl, mix together remaining ingredients except buns and coleslaw; spoon over roast. Cover and bake at 325 degrees for 2-3/4 hours, or until very tender. The pan juices will become a delicious gravy as the roast cooks. Shred roast with 2 forks; stir into juices. Serve beef on buns, topped with coleslaw if desired. Makes 8 to 10 sandwiches.

Adopt an old tradition...tuck a glass pickle ornament among the branches of a decorated tree. When it's time to pack away the decorations, whoever finds the pickle gets a small prize!

Gathering with Family & Friends

Edith's Chipped Ham Bar-B-Q

Dianne Ables
North Potomac, MD

My mother used to make these sandwiches around the holidays, and my family always looked forward to these savory treats. The small slider buns that are so popular now are perfect for this.

1/2 c. brown sugar, packed
1/2 c. vinegar
12-oz. bottle chili sauce
1/2 t. dry mustard
1/2 c. celery, finely chopped
1/2 c. onion, finely chopped
1-1/2 lbs. chipped or thinly sliced deli ham
10 to 12 slider buns, split

In a large heavy saucepan, combine all ingredients except ham and buns. Simmer over low heat for one hour, stirring occasionally. Add ham; mix well and heat through. Serve ham on buns. Makes 10 to 12 sandwiches.

I'll be home for Christmas,
You can plan on me
Please have snow and mistletoe
And presents on the tree...

–Kim Gannon

161

Baked Cod Dinner

Regina Vining
Warwick, RI

My mother always prepared the traditional Italian Feast of Seven Fishes for our Christmas Eve dinner. I like to keep things simple, but fish is still a must! This dinner is delicious and easy, served with a zesty tossed salad and some warm Italian bread.

1 T. olive oil
14-oz. can artichoke hearts, drained
2 c. cherry tomatoes
1/2 c. jumbo black olives, halved
1 green pepper, cut into strips
4 cloves garlic, crushed
1 T. fennel seed
1-1/2 lbs. cod or halibut fillets, thawed if frozen
2 T. capers, drained
zest and juice of 1 orange
salt and pepper to taste

Drizzle olive oil over a 15"x10" jelly-roll pan. Evenly arrange artichokes, tomatoes, olives and green pepper on pan; sprinkle with garlic and fennel seed. Cut fish fillets into serving-size portions and arrange over vegetables. Sprinkle with capers, orange zest and juice; season with salt and pepper. Bake, uncovered, at 450 degrees for 30 minutes, or until vegetables are tender and fish flakes easily with a fork. Serves 4.

A real conversation starter...ask your older relatives about their earliest holiday memories. Did they have a Christmas tree? How was it decorated? Do they remember setting out cookies & milk for Santa? Don't miss the opportunity to preserve these precious memories on video.

Gathering with Family & Friends

Garlic-Brown Sugar Glazed Salmon

Mary Ann Hodges
Williamsburg, VA

My daughter loves this salmon, so we serve it for special occasions and whenever we want to treat ourselves. Scrumptious!

2-lb. salmon fillet
salt and pepper to taste
1/4 c. brown sugar, packed
1/4 c. soy sauce
2 T. olive oil

juice of 1 lemon
3 cloves garlic, minced
1 t. salt
1/2 t. pepper
Garnish: lemon slices

Place salmon on an aluminum foil-lined baking sheet; season with salt and pepper. Fold up the sides of foil around the salmon; set aside. In a small bowl, whisk together remaining ingredients except garnish; spoon mixture over salmon. Top salmon with another piece of foil; crimp edges to seal. Bake at 350 degrees for 20 minutes, or until salmon flakes easily and is cooked through. Uncover; baste salmon with pan drippings. Place pan under broiler for 3 to 5 minutes; broil until golden. Garnish with lemon slices. Serves 4.

For a no-fuss Christmas dinner, set out a make-ahead buffet of sliced baked ham or roast turkey, rolls or bread and a favorite side dish warming in a slow cooker. For dessert, a platter of Christmas cookies, of course. Relax...you'll enjoy the day too!

I'll Be Home for
Christmas
Cookbook

Slow-Cooker Beef Burgundy

Linda Behling
Cecil, PA

With the busy holidays, we sometimes don't have time to make special meals for our families. After a busy work day or shopping day, you can serve this up from your slow cooker in no time at all. My family loves it and the welcome smells that greet you when you walk through the door are amazing!

3 T. butter
3 lbs. beef rump roast, cut
    into 1-1/2 inch cubes
1 onion, sliced
1 clove garlic, minced
1/4 c. all-purpose flour
10-1/2 oz. can beef broth
1 c. dry red wine or beef broth

2 T. tomato paste
1/2 lb. mushrooms, halved
1 t. dried thyme
1 bay leaf
1 t. salt
1/4 t. pepper
cooked egg noodles

Melt butter in a skillet over medium-high heat; brown roast on all sides. Transfer roast to a 4-quart slow cooker. Add onion and garlic to drippings in skillet; sauté until tender, stirring often. Stir in flour; cook, stirring constantly, for one minute. Slowly stir in broth, wine or broth and tomato paste. Simmer for one to 2 minutes, until sauce coats the back of a wooden spoon. Stir in remaining ingredients except noodles. Spoon mixture over roast in slow cooker. Cover and cook on low setting for 8 hours, or until beef is tender. Discard bay leaf. To serve, ladle beef mixture over noodles. Serves 6.

Create a cozy glow in a non-working fireplace. Fill it with an arrangement of glowing pillar candles, either real or battery-operated.

Gathering with *Family & Friends*

Pork Roast With Plum Sauce

Sandy Coffey
Cincinnati, OH

I love pork roast for special occasions. This recipe is from my sister-in-law Patricia, who is a great cook. I think it is the plum sauce that makes it special. For a different flair, use apricot preserves.

3-lb. pork loin roast
1/2 t. garlic salt
1/2 t. salt
3/4 c. onion, chopped
2 T. butter
12-oz. jar plum preserves

6-oz. can frozen lemonade
    concentrate
2/3 c. chili sauce
1 T. soy sauce
2 t. mustard
1 t. ground ginger

Place roast in a lightly greased 13"x9" baking pan. Season with salts; set aside. In a saucepan over medium heat, sauté onion in butter. Stir in remaining ingredients; heat through and spoon over roast. Bake, uncovered, at 350 degrees for about 1-1/2 hours, or allow 30 to 45 minutes cooking time per pound. Baste with sauce in pan several times while pork is cooking. Makes 6 servings.

Recall simpler times at Christmas with charming table favors. Fill mini brown paper bags with a juicy orange, a popcorn ball, nuts for cracking and old-fashioned hard candies. Tie with yarn and set one at each place. So sweet!

Baked Spaghetti Casserole

*Katie Bonomo
Ogden, IL*

*Every time I make this for someone new, they always ask
for the recipe. It's a nice alternative to lasagna.*

16-oz. pkg. spaghetti, uncooked
1 lb. ground beef
1 lb. ground pork sausage
1 onion, chopped
4 cloves garlic, minced
1 t. garlic powder
48-oz. jar traditional or
   mushroom spaghetti sauce
15-oz. can sliced mushrooms,
   drained

1-1/2 c. small-curd cottage
   cheese
8-oz. pkg. cream cheese,
   softened
1 egg, beaten
1 T. Italian seasoning
16-oz. pkg. shredded mozzarella
   cheese, divided

Cook spaghetti according to package directions; drain. Meanwhile, in
a large skillet over medium heat, cook beef, sausage, onion and garlic
until meats are no longer pink. Drain; stir in garlic powder, sauce and
mushrooms. Simmer for 20 to 30 minutes, stirring occasionally. In a
bowl, stir together cottage cheese, cream cheese, egg and Italian
seasoning; set aside. Spray a 13"x9" baking pan with non-stick olive oil
spray. Spread 3/4 cup sauce in the bottom of pan. Layer with half each
of noodles, cream cheese mixture, beef mixture and mozzarella cheese.
Repeat layering. Bake, uncovered, at 350 degrees for 30 to 40 minutes,
until hot and bubbly. Makes 8 servings.

Make-ahead casseroles are
perfect after a day of Christmas
shopping. For an easy side, whip
up a marinated salad to keep in
the fridge...just cut up crunchy
veggies and toss with zesty
Italian salad dressing.

Gathering with Family & Friends

Sautéed Shrimp Kiev

Gail Hageman
Albion, ME

I have been making this dish for about 30 years. It is a very nice dinner for family, and special enough for guests. A healthier alternative to shrimp scampi!

16-oz. pkg. angel hair pasta, uncooked
4 T. butter or olive oil, divided
2 green peppers, cut into strips
2 cloves garlic, chopped and divided
1 lb. uncooked medium or large shrimp, peeled and cleaned
1 t. dried oregano
1 t. dried tarragon
1/2 t. salt
16 cherry tomatoes
1/2 c. white wine or chicken broth
1 T. lemon juice

Cook pasta according to package directions; drain. Meanwhile, add 2 tablespoons butter or oil to a skillet over medium heat. Add green peppers; sauté until tender-crisp. Just before peppers are done, add half the garlic; don't allow garlic to burn. Remove peppers from skillet; set aside. Add remaining butter or oil to skillet. Add shrimp, seasonings and remaining garlic. Sauté until shrimp is slightly firm. Stir in tomatoes, wine or broth and lemon juice. Cover and simmer for 2 to 4 minutes, until shrimp is opaque. Return peppers to skillet; heat through. To serve, ladle shrimp mixture over cooked pasta. Serves 4.

While you're adding the finishing touches to a holiday meal, set out a wooden bowl of whole walnuts or pecans and a nutcracker for guests. It'll double as a party activity and a light snack...before you know it, dinner is served!

Red & Green Orzo

Danika Wilson
Anchorage, AK

Growing up vegetarian, I often envied the beautiful roasted meats that starred on the holiday dinner table. This rich dish lends itself to being a special Christmas dish, thanks to the festive red and green colors of the vegetables. If you prefer, use regular diced tomatoes instead of the fire-roasted variety...or turn up the heat with a can of diced tomatoes and green chiles!

16-oz. pkg. orzo pasta,
   uncooked
1 T. butter
1 T. olive oil
1/2 c. onion, minced
3 cloves garlic, minced

2 c. frozen peas
14-1/2 oz. can fire-roasted
   diced tomatoes
1 c. half-and-half
salt and pepper to taste
1 c. grated Parmesan cheese

Cook pasta according to package directions. Drain, reserving cooking water. Meanwhile, in a deep skillet over medium heat, melt butter with oil. Add onion and garlic; cook until translucent. Add peas and tomatoes with juice; cook for about 3 minutes, or until warmed through. Stir in half-and-half and cooked pasta; toss to combine. Season with salt and pepper; sprinkle with Parmesan cheese. Let stand until cheese melts. If sauce seems too thick, stir in some of the reserved cooking water until a smooth consistency is reached and pasta is evenly coated. Makes 6 servings.

Try a potluck for Christmas Eve...everyone brings their favorite dish and no one has to do all the work!

Gathering with *Family & Friends*

Mémé's Pork Pie

Theresa Chaloux
Portsmouth, NH

We all looked forward to my Mémé's pork pie, which she made for our family every Thanksgiving and Christmas. She took the time and patience to make the perfect pie for our holiday.

3/4 c. onion, chopped
1 T. oil
poultry seasoning, salt and
    pepper to taste
1 lb. ground pork

1 lb. ground beef
2 to 3 potatoes, peeled and diced
2 9-inch pie crusts, unbaked
2 to 3 t. milk

In a large skillet over medium heat, cook onion in oil until translucent. Sprinkle with seasonings; add pork and beef. Cook over medium heat until browned; drain. Meanwhile, cover potatoes with water in a saucepan; bring to a boil over high heat. Cook until potatoes are fork-tender; drain. Add potatoes to beef mixture; set aside to cool. Arrange one pie crust in a 9" pie plate. Spoon beef mixture into crust. Cover with remaining crust; crimp edges to seal. With a knife tip, cut several vents in crust. Brush crust lightly with milk. Cover the edges of pie crust with strips of aluminum foil to prevent burning. Bake at 350 degrees for 35 to 40 minutes, until bubbly and crust is golden. Makes 8 servings.

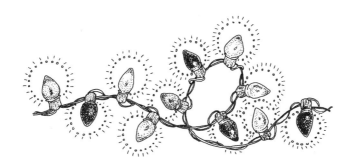

Do you have a child returning home for the holidays?
Give her a rousing welcome by decorating her
bedroom with twinkly colored lights!

Grandma Marie's Wonderful Glazed Ham

Jayne Porter
Dittmer, MO

When I was a little girl, every year at Christmas and Easter my Grandma Marie would bake a huge ham for dinner. She always made a wonderful glaze for her baked ham. Through the years, my mother and I have used Grandma Marie's recipe...now my daughter is the fourth generation to use it. You can use the size and type of ham you like, and omit the pineapple and cherries, if you prefer.

18 to 20-lb. fully-cooked ham
30 to 60 whole cloves
1 to 2 20-oz. cans pineapple chunks, drained and juice reserved

10-oz. jar maraschino cherries, drained
2 c. brown sugar, packed
2 to 3 t. ground cloves

With a sharp knife, score the skin on top of ham into one-inch diamond shapes. Push whole cloves into the centers of diamonds. Fasten pineapple chunks to top of ham, using a wooden toothpick for each; add a cherry to each toothpick. Place ham in a roasting pan; set aside. In a saucepan, combine brown sugar, reserved pineapple juice and ground cloves; add a little water if needed. Cook and stir over medium heat; bring to a boil. Simmer over low heat for 15 minutes, or until thickened. Spoon glaze all over ham until well covered; tent ham with aluminum foil. Bake at 325 degrees for 2 to 2-1/2 hours, depending on size of ham. Remove from oven; cover with glaze again, along with pan drippings. Bake another 10 minutes. Remove from oven; cover with glaze again. Bake another 10 minutes, or until ham is heated through and a meat thermometer inserted in the center reads 140 degrees. Remove ham to a platter; slice and serve. Makes about 20 servings.

For the easiest napkin rings, tie a colorful ribbon bow around napkins and tuck in a sprig of greenery.

Gathering with Family & Friends

Oven Beef Stew

Lynn Huntley
Mountain, WI

I have been making this recipe for many years. My family looks forward to it on a chilly day. It smells so good as it simmers for hours in the oven. Serve with thick slices of buttered bread.

3 to 4 T. oil
3 to 4 lbs. beef chuck or sirloin
   roast, cut into large cubes
6 potatoes, peeled and quartered
6 carrots, peeled and chopped
4 stalks celery, with leafy tops,
   chopped
1/2 lb. mushrooms, quartered
1 to 2 onions, coarsely chopped

1 green pepper, coarsely chopped
6 cloves garlic, pressed
4 c. beef broth
2 c. red wine or beef broth
6-oz. can tomato paste
1/4 c. molasses
4 to 6 bay leaves
salt and pepper to taste

Heat oil in a heavy skillet over medium-high heat. Working in batches, brown beef on all sides; drain. Transfer beef to a large roasting pan; add remaining ingredients. Stir well. Add roasting pan lid or cover with aluminum foil. Bake at 300 degrees for 3 to 4 hours, stirring occasionally. Discard bay leaves at serving time. Serves 8.

Fill a mesh tea ball with dried bay leaves or other whole spices as a small gift for a favorite cook. Hung on the side of the pan, it makes removing the spices a snap.

Creamy Ziti Casserole

Shirley Howie
Foxboro, MA

I often make this dish during the holidays, when it gets busy around here. It is easy to put together, and leftovers taste even better the next day! It's a real time-saver and also freezes well for a quick, ready-made meal when time is short.

8-oz. pkg. ziti pasta, uncooked
1/2 lb. ground beef
1/2 c. onion, chopped
1 clove garlic, minced
15-1/2 oz. jar pasta sauce
1/8 t. pepper

15-oz. container ricotta cheese
1-1/2 c. shredded mozzarella
  cheese, divided
1/2 t. salt
1/4 c. grated Parmesan cheese

Cook pasta according to package directions, just until tender; drain. Meanwhile, in a large skillet over medium-high heat, cook beef, onion and garlic for 4 minutes, or until beef is lightly browned. Stir in pasta sauce and pepper. Reduce heat to medium-low; simmer for 5 minutes. In a large bowl, combine ricotta cheese, one cup mozzarella cheese and salt. Add pasta sauce mixture and cooked pasta; stir just until pasta is coated. Spoon into a lightly greased 2-quart casserole dish. Top with remaining mozzarella cheese and Parmesan cheese. Bake, uncovered, at 350 degrees for 20 minutes, or until heated through. Makes 4 servings.

Dress up any pasta dish for the holidays...
choose bowtie pasta!

Gathering with
Family & Friends

Em's Slow-Cooker Chicken

Emilie Britton
New Bremen, OH

Everyone loves this chicken with its light, creamy gravy. Good with mashed potatoes or steamed rice alongside pan-fried green beans... yum! This recipe is great made with pork chops too.

3/4 c. all-purpose flour, divided
1/2 t. dry mustard
1/4 t. seasoned salt
1/2 t. garlic-pepper blend

4 boneless, skinless chicken
    breasts
2 T. oil
14-1/2 oz. can chicken broth

In a large plastic zipping bag, combine 1/2 cup flour and seasonings. Add chicken to bag, one piece at a time; shake to coat and set aside. Heat oil in a large skillet over medium heat; brown chicken on both sides. Transfer chicken to a 5-quart slow cooker. Place remaining flour in a bowl; whisk in broth until smooth. Pour over chicken. Cover and cook on low setting for 3-1/2 to 4 hours, until tender. Remove to a serving plate; cover to keep warm. Whisk juices in slow cooker until smooth; serve with chicken. Serves 4.

Pork Chops & Cola

Joyce Borrill
Utica, NY

It's hard to believe, but this quick & easy recipe is truly delicious! You may use chicken pieces instead of pork chops, if desired.

1 c. onion, sliced
2 T. oil or butter
6 to 8 pork chops

1 c. catsup
12-oz. can regular cola

In a large skillet over medium heat, sauté onion in oil or butter. Spoon onion into a greased 2-quart casserole dish; set aside. Brown pork chops in drippings in skillet. Transfer chops to casserole dish. Mix together catsup and cola; spoon over chops. Bake, uncovered, at 375 degrees for 45 minutes. Makes 6 to 8 servings.

Shrimp Penne Alfredo

Beverley Williams
San Antonio, TX

This is one of my family's favorite dishes...I like the combination of flavors. Either homemade or jarred Alfredo sauce may be used. Serve with hot garlic bread.

16-oz. pkg. penne pasta,
  uncooked
3 slices bacon
1 c. sliced mushrooms
2 c. frozen peas, thawed
  and drained

2 4-oz. cans tiny shrimp,
  drained
1 roma tomato, diced
3 c. Alfredo sauce

Cook pasta according to package directions; drain. Meanwhile, cook bacon in a skillet over medium heat until crisp; drain on a paper towel. Add mushrooms to drippings in skillet; sauté until tender. In a large microwave-safe bowl, combine cooked pasta, crumbled bacon, mushrooms and remaining ingredients. Microwave on high for one minute, or until heated through. Makes 4 to 6 servings.

Rebecca's Scalloped Oysters

Paula Weaver
Steeleville, IL

My friend from Kentucky gave me this recipe years ago and it's become a holiday favorite. Easy to fix, and tastes so good.

1 sleeve saltine crackers, crushed
  and divided
2 8-oz. cans whole oysters

1 c. half-and-half
2 T. butter, diced

In a buttered one-quart casserole dish, layer half of crushed crackers and one can oysters with juice. Repeat layering. Cover with half-and-half; dot with butter. Bake, uncovered, at 350 degrees for 30 to 40 minutes, until hot and bubbly. Serves 8.

Gathering with Family & Friends

Simple Chicken Piccata

Patricia Reitz
Winchester, VA

Chicken piccata is one of those really quick, one-pot dishes every home cook should know how to make! The thin chicken breasts cook in minutes, and the buttery lemon and caper sauce is full of flavor. I love that I can walk in the door and have it on the table in less than 30 minutes. The recipe makes a lot of pan sauce, which is wonderful served over steamed rice or sopped up with crusty bread.

2 boneless, skinless chicken
    breasts, cut in half
1/4 c. all-purpose flour
3 T. butter, divided
2 T. olive oil
1 c. chicken broth

1 c. white wine or chicken broth
juice of 1 lemon
1 t. capers, drained
Optional: salt and pepper to taste
Garnish: lemon slices, chopped
    fresh parsley

Pound chicken pieces to about 1/4-inch thickness. Dredge chicken in flour; set aside. Melt 2 tablespoons butter with oil in a very large skillet. Sauté chicken until golden on both sides; remove from pan. Add broth and wine or broth to drippings in pan, stirring to dissolve all the browned bits. If desired, skim away any solids that don't dissolve. Stir in lemon juice and capers. Cook until reduced by half, stirring occasionally. Season pan sauce with salt and pepper, if desired; whisk in remaining butter. Return chicken to skillet; baste with pan sauce to gently reheat chicken. Garnish as desired. Serves 2.

Vintage salt & pepper shakers add a touch of holiday cheer to any table and a smile to guests' faces.

Unique Broiled Sandwich

Joann Eicher
Topeka, KS

Mama made this special treat for us to come home to, after a cold evening of ice skating! This tasted so good on a cold winter night.

6 to 8 hamburger buns, split
mustard to taste
1 lb. lean ground beef
1/4 c. catsup

1 egg, beaten
1 t. prepared horseradish
salt and pepper to taste

Spread cut sides of bun halves with mustard out to the edges; set aside. In a bowl, mix together uncooked beef and remaining ingredients. Spread beef mixture on cut sides of bun halves with a fork, making ridges in the beef with the fork. Place on a broiler pan. Broil for 4 to 5 minutes, until beef is browned. Makes 12 to 16 open-face sandwiches.

Grilled Pepper Jack Sandwiches

Amy Thomason Hunt
Traphill, NC

I adapted this from another recipe to suit our tastes...we like it!

4 T. butter, softened
2 t. taco seasoning mix

8 slices bread
4 slices Pepper Jack cheese

Thoroughly blend butter and taco seasoning. Spread butter mixture on one side of each slice of bread. Heat a large skillet or griddle over medium heat. Place 4 bread slices in skillet, butter-side down; top each with a cheese slice. Top with remaining bread slices, butter-side up. Cook until bread is golden and cheese is melted, turning once. Makes 4 sandwiches.

After a hearty meal, enjoy a frosty walk around the neighborhood to enjoy the twinkling Christmas lights.

Gathering with Family & Friends

Better-Than-the-Deli Reubens

Sandra Sullivan
Aurora, CO

*We love sandwiches with a bowl of hot, steamy soup after a day
on the ski slopes...this one is quick and oh-so yummy!*

12 slices light or dark rye bread
favorite mustard to taste
8-oz. pkg. cream cheese,
  softened
16-oz. can sauerkraut, well
  drained
1 lb. thinly sliced deli corned beef
1 lb. thinly sliced Swiss cheese

Spread one side of bread slices with mustard; set aside. In a bowl,
combine cream cheese and sauerkraut; blend with an electric mixer on
low speed or by hand. Divide corned beef among bread slices; spoon
cream cheese and sauerkraut mixture over corned beef. Top each with a
cheese slice. Arrange on a broiler pan; broil until cheese bubbles. Makes
12 open-face sandwiches.

Making some surprise balls to unwrap on Christmas Eve.
Wrap strips of crepe paper round & round little toys
and candies to form a ball. Everyone will love
unwinding the paper to find the surprises inside!

One-Pan Turkey Dinner

Robin Hill
Rochester, NY

A simple no-fuss way to serve up a festive turkey dinner.

2-lb. pkg. frozen turkey breast
    cutlets, thawed
salt and pepper to taste
1 lb. baby redskin potatoes,
    halved

2 T. olive oil, divided
1/2 lb. green beans, trimmed
1/2 lb. baby carrots
1 T. fresh thyme, chopped
Optional: turkey gravy

Line a rimmed baking sheet with aluminum foil; set a roasting rack on the pan. Season turkey with salt and pepper; place on rack. Bake, uncovered, at 375 degrees on lower oven rack for 45 minutes. Meanwhile, in a large bowl, toss potatoes with one tablespoon oil; season with salt. Arrange potatoes around turkey. Turn oven temperature to 425 degrees; move pan to center oven rack. Bake for another 20 minutes, stirring potatoes occasionally. In same bowl, toss beans and carrots with remaining oil; season with thyme, salt and pepper. Spread beans and carrots around turkey in a single layer. Return to oven; bake for another 20 to 30 minutes, until a meat thermometer inserted into thickest part of turkey reads 165 degrees. To serve, transfer turkey and vegetables to a platter. Serve with gravy, if desired. Serves 6.

Keep the Christmas dinner menu simple, familiar and yummy. Ask your family ahead of time what dishes are special to them. It's a day for tradition and comfort... and you'll be more relaxed too.

Gathering with *Family & Friends*

Grandma's Ham Balls

Kimberly Redeker
Savoy, IL

These ham balls are a special treat that has been the main dish for many a Christmas Eve at Grandma's house. I even requested them for my college graduation party! They are super-easy to make, satisfy all kinds of tastes and freeze easily. I served them last Christmas Eve, and they were half gone before I could even get a photo of them!

1-1/4 lbs. smoked ham
1-1/4 lbs. lean pork
1 egg, beaten

1 c. dry bread crumbs
1 c. milk

In a food processor or chopper, grind together ham and pork. Transfer to a large bowl; mix with remaining ingredients. Roll into balls, about 1-1/2 to 2 inches in diameter. Place ham balls in a lightly greased 13"x9" baking pan. Spoon Sauce over top. Bake, uncovered, at 350 degrees for one hour. Turn balls over; bake for about one more hour, basting with sauce from pan if they start to look dry. Serves 12.

Sauce:

1 c. brown sugar, packed
1/2 c. sugar

1/2 c. vinegar
1 t. dry mustard

Mix together all ingredients in a saucepan. Cook over medium-low heat, stirring often, until sugars dissolve.

Gather up the little mittens that the children have outgrown...they make such a sweet decoration for a front-door wreath.

White Bean Cassoulet

Mary Bettuchy
Saint Robert, MO

There is nothing better on a dreary day than the aroma of this cassoulet in the oven...or any day, for that matter! It is one of my favorite go-to comfort food recipes.

16-oz. pkg. dried Great Northern
  beans, rinsed and sorted
1 onion, diced
5 T. extra-virgin olive oil, divided
2 cloves garlic, minced
6-1/2 c. vegetable or chicken
  broth
1 bay leaf
1 eggplant, peeled and cubed
3 tomatoes, chopped
salt and pepper to taste
1 c. Italian-flavored dry bread
  crumbs
1 c. shredded Parmesan cheese

Place dried beans in a large stockpot; add enough water to cover by 2 inches and soak overnight. Drain beans; set aside. In the same stockpot over medium heat, sauté onion in one tablespoon oil for about 5 minutes, until softened. Add garlic; sauté one minute more. Add broth, drained beans and bay leaf to stockpot; bring to a boil over high heat. Reduce heat to medium-low. Simmer for about one hour, until most of the liquid has been absorbed and beans are thick and creamy. Discard bay leaf. Meanwhile, in a bowl, toss eggplant and tomato with 2 tablespoons oil. Spread in a single layer on a parchment paper-lined rimmed baking sheet. Season lightly with salt and pepper. Bake at 400 degrees for 15 minutes, or until soft. Add eggplant mixture to beans; mix gently. Transfer bean mixture to a greased 13"x9" baking pan. In another bowl, combine bread crumbs, cheese and remaining oil; mix well. Mixture should be slightly moist but still crumbly; add more oil if needed. Sprinkle bread crumb mixture over bean mixture. Bake, uncovered, at 400 degrees for about 15 to 20 minutes, until crumbs are golden. Makes 6 to 8 servings.

A family is a circle of friends who love you.
–Unknown

Gathering with Family & Friends

Baked Chimichangas

Diane Skidmore
Visalia, CA

I have been making this dish for years. It's a very versatile recipe! These chimis are meatless, but sometimes I use leftover cooked chicken, pork or beef as a substitute for the beans. Double the recipe for a crowd. Serve with a chopped salad...so good and easy!

29-oz. can pinto beans, drained and rinsed
4-oz. can sliced black olives, drained
4-oz. can diced green chiles
1 c. shredded coleslaw mix with carrots
1 c. shredded sharp Cheddar cheese
1 c. mild or medium salsa
6 10-inch flour tortillas, warmed
Garnish: additional salsa, sour cream, sliced green onions

In a large bowl, combine beans, olives, chiles, coleslaw, cheese and salsa. Spoon mixture down the center of warmed tortillas, dividing evenly. Fold over both sides of each tortilla toward the center; fold in one end and roll tightly to enclose filling. Place filled tortillas seam-side down in a 15"x12" jelly-roll pan coated with non-stick vegetable spray. Bake at 425 degrees for about 15 minutes, until crisp and golden. Garnish as desired. Makes 6 servings.

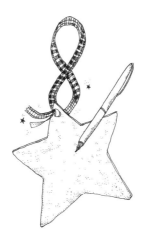

Start a sweet new tradition at your holiday dinner... hand out paper star cut-outs and have each person write down what they're happiest for since last Christmas.

No-Peek Beef Tips

Tina Butler
Royse City, TX

This is definitely my go-to recipe, because it always turns out well. It's always a hit, any time I make it, and so foolproof you can't mess it up. The house smells so delightful while the beef tips are baking. Serve over steamed rice, mashed potatoes or cooked egg noodles.

2 lbs. beef tenderloin tips or
    stew beef cubes
10-3/4 oz. can cream of
    mushroom soup
1 c. ginger ale or water

1-1/4 oz. pkg. onion soup mix
0.87-oz. pkg. brown gravy mix
4-oz. can sliced mushrooms,
    drained

Spread beef cubes evenly in a lightly greased 13"x9" baking pan; set aside. In a large bowl, combine remaining ingredients except mushrooms; mix well and spoon over beef. Add mushrooms and stir to coat. Cover with aluminum foil. Bake at 300 degrees for 3 hours. Do not remove foil until done. Serves 6 to 8.

Take it easy when planning holiday dinners...stick to tried & true recipes that you know will be delicious! Guests are often just as happy with simple comfort foods as with the most elegant gourmet meal.

Holiday Desserts
for Sharing

I'll Be Home for
Christmas
Cookbook

Crispy Sugar Cookies

Karen Antonides
Gahanna, OH

This was my mom's favorite sugar cookie recipe. The cookies have a hint of lemon and nutmeg that makes them special...they're great to dunk in hot coffee or tea! Assorted sugar sprinkles make these cookies really sparkle on a holiday cookie tray.

1 c. butter, softened
1-1/4 c. sugar
3 eggs, beaten
1/2 t. nutmeg
1/2 t. lemon extract
3-1/2 c. all-purpose flour

2 t. cream of tartar
1 t. baking soda
1 t. salt
Garnish: sparkling sugar or
   candy sprinkles

In a large bowl, combine butter and sugar; beat with an electric mixer on medium speed until blended. Beat in eggs, nutmeg and extract; set aside. In another bowl, combine remaining ingredients except garnish. Add flour mixture to butter mixture, one cup at a time; mix well. Divide dough into 2 balls. On a floured surface, roll out each ball to 1/8-inch thick. Cut out cookies with cookie cutters; place on greased baking sheets. Top with sparkling sugar or sprinkles. Bake at 375 degrees for 8 to 10 minutes. Makes about 4 dozen.

Here's an easy trick to help cut-out cookie shapes bake up neatly. Place cookies on a parchment paper-lined baking sheet and pop into the fridge for 10 to 15 minutes, then bake.

Holiday Desserts for Sharing

Merry Meringues

Cathy Hillier
Salt Lake City, UT

We love these crunchy, delicate cookies, and they're really easy to make. The red and green colors are perfect for a cookie tray.

4 egg whites
1/4 t. cream of tartar
3/4 c. sugar

3-oz. pkg. lime gelatin mix
3-oz. pkg. strawberry gelatin mix

In a deep bowl, combine egg whites and cream of tartar. Beat with an electric mixer on high speed for 5 minutes, or until soft peaks form. Gradually beat in sugar, one tablespoon at a time; beat until stiff peaks form. Drop mixture by tablespoonfuls onto 2 parchment paper-covered baking sheets. Lightly sprinkle meringues on one baking sheet with lime gelatin mix; sprinkle meringues on the other baking sheet with cherry gelatin mix. Bake at 225 degrees for 50 minutes. Turn oven off. Prop oven door open slightly; leave meringues in oven for one hour, or until completely cool. Store at room temperature in an airtight container. Makes 2 dozen.

For a special Christmas dessert, bake your favorite layer cake, decorate it with birthday candles and sing "Happy Birthday" to Jesus!

Peppermint Butter Balls

Sharon Buxton
Warsaw, OH

When I was growing up in northeastern Ohio, Grandma's peppermint butter balls were always a must for Christmas. Easy to make, the most difficult part used to be the tedious crushing of candy canes, but now, with pre-packaged peppermint bits, it's a snap! An added bonus is the peppermint smell of Christmas wafting through the house.

1/2 c. butter	2 t. baking powder
3/4 c. powdered sugar	1/2 t. salt
1 t. vanilla extract	1/4 c. crushed peppermint
1/4 t. peppermint extract	candy bits
1 egg, beaten	Garnish: additional sugar
1-1/2 c. all-purpose flour	

In a large bowl, blend butter and powdered sugar. Add extracts and egg; beat until well mixed and set aside. In another bowl, sift together flour, baking powder and salt. Add flour mixture to butter mixture along with crushed peppermints; mix well. Cover and chill at least 2 hours. Form dough into 1-1/2 inch balls; roll in sugar. Arrange on greased and floured baking sheets, 2 inches apart. Bake at 350 degrees for 10 minutes, or until lightly golden. Makes 3 dozen.

Don't forget the camera on family cookie baking day! Snapshots of children's little hands cutting out cookies, sweet faces smudged with frosting and gorgeous platters of decorated cookies will be cherished for years to come.

Holiday Desserts for Sharing

Ruby's Buttermilk Pecan Candy

Cassie Hooker
La Porte, TX

This is a recipe my mother used to make for us every year at Christmas when we were growing up. We only got this candy once a year, so we always looked forward to Mother's holiday baking! Don't make this when it is damp or humid outside, it won't set right.

2 c. sugar
1 c. buttermilk
1/4 c. margarine
2 T. white corn syrup

1/2 t. baking soda
1 t. vanilla extract
1 c. chopped pecans

In a large, heavy saucepan, combine all ingredients except vanilla and pecans. Cook over medium heat until boiling; stop stirring. Cook until mixture comes to the soft-ball stage, or 234 to 243 degrees on a candy thermometer. Remove from heat; add vanilla but don't stir. Let the pan cool for about 10 minutes. Beat with whisk for about 5 minutes, until mixture changes to a creamy texture and sets up in the pan. Add pecans; return to very low heat. Stir until soft enough to drop onto wax paper by teaspoonfuls. Let stand until set. Makes 2 dozen.

Quick Candy Bark

Kathy Grashoff
Fort Wayne, IN

This is beautiful wrapped in cellophane and tied with ribbon for gifts. Choose your small candies according to the season! Crushed peppermints work well too.

12-oz. pkg. white candy coating
1 c. mini candy-coated chocolates

Optional: candy sprinkles, melted
dark chocolate for drizzling

Melt candy coating according to package directions. Spread evenly on a parchment paper-lined 15"x10" jelly-roll pan. Arrange candies and sprinkles as desired. Let stand until firm, about 30 minutes. Drizzle with dark chocolate, if desired. Turn bark out of pan; peel off paper and break into chunks. Wrap in cellophane or store in an airtight container. Makes about one pound.

Grandma's Spicy Thins

Jenna Hord
Warsaw, OH

Grandma made these cookies every Christmas, and we were allowed to eat them for breakfast. She gave my sister and me a tin filled with these cookies, with her recipe attached. Now I make them every Christmas and Valentine's Day, and I always think of my grandma!

1 c. margarine	2 t. baking soda
1-1/2 c. sugar	2 t. ground ginger
1 egg, beaten	2 t. ground cloves
2 T. dark corn syrup	2 t. cinnamon
3 c. all-purpose flour	

In a large bowl, blend margarine and sugar. Blend in egg and corn syrup; set aside. In another bowl, sift together flour, baking soda and spices. Add flour mixture to margarine mixture; stir well. Cover and chill until firm. On a floured surface, roll out to 1/8-inch thick; cut with assorted cookie cutters. Place on greased baking sheets. Bake at 400 degrees for 5 to 8 minutes. Cool; frost with Icing, if desired. Makes about 6 dozen.

Icing:

1 c. powdered sugar	1 to 2 T. milk
1/2 t. vanilla extract	Optional: few drops food coloring

Combine powdered sugar, vanilla and enough milk to make a spreadable consistency. Stir in food coloring, if desired.

Wrapping up a care package of cookies to mail?
Choose sturdy cookies that won't crumble easily. Drop
cookies, brownies and bar cookies are great travelers,
while frosted or filled cookies may be too fragile.

Holiday Desserts for Sharing

Chocolate Crinkle Cookies

Hollie Moots
Marysville, OH

For me, it wouldn't be Christmas without these cookies! I can remember making them with my mom and grandma when I was a little girl, and I've continued to make them with my kids as well. So chocolatey and good!

1/2 c. shortening
4 sqs. unsweetened baking
   chocolate, melted
2 c. sugar
4 eggs, beaten

2 t. vanilla extract
2 c. all-purpose flour
2 t. baking powder
1/2 t. salt
Garnish: powdered sugar

Mix shortening, melted chocolate and sugar in a large bowl. Beat in eggs, one at a time, until well blended. Add vanilla; set aside. In another bowl, combine flour, baking powder and salt; stir into chocolate mixture. Cover and refrigerate several hours or overnight. Shape dough into one-inch balls; roll in powdered sugar. Arrange balls on greased or parchment paper-lined baking sheets, 2 inches apart. Bake at 350 degrees for 10 to 12 minutes, until set on the outside. Do not overbake. Makes 3 dozen.

A drizzle of chocolate makes any home-baked cookie or candy extra special. Simply place chocolate chips in a small plastic zipping bag and microwave briefly, until melted. Snip off a tiny corner and squeeze to drizzle...afterwards, just toss away the bag.

French Apple Bread Pudding

Jennie Gist
Gooseberry Patch

Dad just loved this bread pudding! It's warm and comforting.
A drizzle of caramel topping would be a delicious addition.

3 eggs
14-oz. can sweetened condensed
   milk
3 apples, peeled, cored and finely
   chopped
1-3/4 c. hot water
1/4 c. butter, melted

1 t. cinnamon
1 t. vanilla extract
4 c. French bread, crusts trimmed
   and cubed
Optional: 1/2 c. raisins
Garnish: vanilla ice cream or
   whipped cream

Beat eggs in a large bowl; add condensed milk, apples, water, butter, cinnamon and vanilla. Fold in bread and raisins, if desired; stir until bread is completely moistened. Spoon into a buttered 9"x9" baking pan. Bake at 350 degrees for 50 to 55 minutes, until a knife tip inserted near center tests clean. Cool slightly. Serve warm, garnished as desired. Serves 6 to 8.

When you go out on Christmas Eve to attend church services or see the Christmas lights, share a plate of homemade cookies with your local fire house or police station...such a neighborly gesture.

Pumpkin Crunch Cobbler

Andrea Heyart
Savannah, TX

Whenever I make this yummy dessert, the smell of pumpkin spice fills the whole house! I put my spin on a recipe from an old church cookbook my aunt gave me years ago.

2 eggs, beaten
15-oz. can pumpkin
1-1/2 c. evaporated milk
3.4-oz. pkg. instant vanilla
   pudding mix
2 T. pumpkin pie spice

3/4 c. biscuit baking mix
3.4-oz. pkg. instant butterscotch
   pudding mix
1/3 c. toffee baking bits
1/2 c. butter, melted

In a large bowl, combine eggs, pumpkin, evaporated milk, dry vanilla pudding mix and spice. Beat until creamy and well combined. Pour into a lightly greased 9"x9" baking pan; set aside. In a separate bowl, stir together baking mix, dry pudding mix and toffee pieces. Mix well; add melted butter and toss well until crumbly. Sprinkle butterscotch mixture over pumpkin mixture. Bake at 350 degrees for 45 to 50 minutes, until set in the center. Makes 9 servings.

Whip up some snow ice cream...it's creamy and oh-so easy. Beat one cup heavy cream until soft peaks form, then fold in 4 cups freshly fallen snow. Add sugar and vanilla to taste...enjoy immediately!

Apple Pie in a Goblet

Mary Ann Dell
Phoenixville, PA

*This recipe is a simple version of apple pie that's scrumptious.
It's been a family favorite ever since the first time I tried it. Twist
a bit of sparkly garland around the stems of the goblets for a
pretty presentation.*

3 tart apples, peeled, cored
   and coarsely chopped
1/4 c. sugar
1/4 c. water
3/4 t. cinnamon

1/4 t. nutmeg
12 shortbread cookies, crushed
2 c. vanilla ice cream
Garnish: whipped cream

In a large saucepan over medium heat, combine apples, sugar, water
and spices. Bring to a boil; reduce heat to medium-low. Cover and
simmer for 10 minutes, or until apples are tender. Uncover; cook for
9 to 11 minutes longer, or until most of the liquid has evaporated.
Remove from heat. In each of 4 glass goblets, layer one tablespoon
cookie crumbs, 1/2 cup ice cream and 1/4 of the warm apple mixture.
Top with remaining cookie crumbs and a dollop of whipped cream.
Serve immediately. Makes 4 servings.

Be sure to pick up a pint or two of ice cream in
cinnamon, peppermint and other delicious seasonal
flavors when they're available...they add that special
touch to holiday meals!

Holiday Desserts for Sharing

Fruited Upside-Down Gingerbread Cake

Denise Webb
Newington, GA

My mother used to make this delicious, old-fashioned dessert in the wintertime. It smells wonderful while baking and tastes so good... it's easy to make, too! It always takes me back to being a little girl at home.

1/2 c. butter, melted
1/2 c. brown sugar, packed
15-oz. can fruit cocktail,
    well drained

15-oz. pkg. gingerbread
    cake mix
Garnish: whipped cream or
    ice cream

Add melted butter to a 9"x9" baking pan; blend in brown sugar. Spread mixture over bottom of pan. Arrange fruit over top; set aside. Prepare gingerbread mix according to package directions; pour batter over fruit. Bake at 350 degrees for 35 to 40 minutes. Immediately turn pan over on a plate; let stand for one to 2 minutes and remove pan. Garnish as desired. Serves 9.

Escalloped Pineapple

PeggyAnn Huffman
Genoa, IL

I make and take this dessert to our neighborhood Christmas party. By the end of the evening, the pan is always scraped clean!

1 c. butter, softened
1-1/2 c. sugar
2 eggs, beaten

20-oz. can pineapple chunks
1/2 c. whipping cream
4 c. bread cubes

In a large bowl, blend butter and sugar. Add eggs; beat well. Fold in undrained pineapple chunks, cream and bread cubes. Mix well and spread in a lightly greased 13"x9" baking pan. Bake at 350 degrees for one hour. Serve warm. Makes 8 servings.

Make sure to have lots of extra chocolate chips, nuts and other baking goodies for sneaking!

Kringla

Laura Fank
Pella, IA

Growing up, it never felt like Christmas until my mom made Kringla. My brother and I could hardly wait for those tasty twists to cool before taking a first bite! When I was a college student, Mom shared those Kringla with my roommates. Now I get to make the Kringla, but somehow, mine never look quite as perfectly twisted as my mom's did!

1/2 c. margarine	3-1/2 c. all-purpose flour
1-1/4 c. sugar	2 t. baking powder
2 eggs, beaten	1/2 t. salt
1 t. vanilla extract	1 c. buttermilk

In a large bowl, combine margarine, sugar, eggs and vanilla. Beat with an electric mixer on medium-high speed until very creamy. Combine flour, baking powder and salt in a separate bowl. Add flour mixture to margarine mixture alternately with buttermilk. Cover and chill overnight. Roll out dough 1/2-inch thick on a floured cloth. Either cut dough into strips and form into figure 8's, or cut with a doughnut cutter and twist to make figure 8's. Place on ungreased baking sheets. Bake at 350 degrees for 8 minutes. Makes 2 to 3 dozen.

Surprises under the tree! Choose a different gift wrap for each member of the family, but keep them a secret 'til it's time to unwrap gifts!

Holiday Desserts for **Sharing**

Old-Fashioned Lace Cookies

Diana Chaney
Olathe, KS

These buttery cookies are crisp and delicate.

1/2 c. butter
1/2 c. plus 2 T. sugar
1 c. plus 2 T. quick-cooking oats,
    uncooked

2 T. all-purpose flour
1 t. baking powder
1 egg, beaten
1/2 c. chopped nuts

Combine butter and sugar in a saucepan over medium heat; stir until butter melts and sugar dissolves. Stir in remaining ingredients; mix well. Drop batter by teaspoonfuls onto aluminum foil-lined baking sheets, 2 inches apart. Bake at 350 degrees for 8 to 10 minutes, watching closely, until golden. Cool completely; remove from pan. Makes 2 to 3 dozen.

Fantastic Peanut Butter Fudge

Nancy Kaiser
York, SC

Everybody's favorite fudge! I have made this every Thanksgiving and Christmas for the last 50 years...I started very young! My mother-in-law gave me this recipe when we first got married. My father-in law probably wouldn't care if we had anything else to eat, as long as we had this fudge. I make sure that he gets it for every holiday.

1 c. butter
12-oz. can evaporated milk
4 c. sugar

7-oz. jar marshmallow creme
1-3/4 c. creamy peanut butter
2 c. chopped peanuts or walnuts

In a heavy kettle over medium heat, combine butter, evaporated milk and sugar. Cook, stirring constantly, until mixture comes to the soft-ball stage, or 234 to 243 degrees on a candy thermometer. Remove from heat. Add remaining ingredients; mix well, but do not scrape sides of pan. Pour into a buttered 15"x10" jelly-roll pan. Let stand until set; cut into squares. Makes about 4 pounds.

Cinnamon Red Hots Divinity

Marilyn Roberts
Alamo, TN

This is so good...it's a different way to make divinity. Makes an excellent candy for Christmas and to give as gifts. I used to make it for Christmas presents and it was always a big hit. Then I lost the recipe for awhile. I was so happy when I found it again!

2-1/2 c. sugar
1/2 c. light corn syrup
1/2 c. water
1/3 c. red cinnamon candies
1/4 t. salt
2 egg whites
1 t. vanilla extract

Lightly spray a baking sheet with non-stick vegetable spray; set aside. In a large, heavy saucepan, combine sugar, corn syrup, water, candies and salt. Cook and stir over medium heat, just until sugar dissolves. Continue cooking without stirring until mixture reaches the soft-ball stage, or about 240 degrees on a candy thermometer. Place egg whites in a deep bowl; beat with an electric mixer on high speed until stiff peaks form. When temperature of sugar mixture reaches 250 degrees, gradually pour it into the egg whites in a steady stream, beating on medium speed. Add vanilla; continue beating for about 5 minutes, until candy holds its shape. Using greased spoons, quickly drop by teaspoonfuls onto prepared pan. Cool completely. Store in airtight containers at room temperature. Makes 3 dozen.

Pure vanilla extract is a must in holiday baking!
Save by purchasing a large bottle at a club store. Ounce
for ounce, it's much cheaper than buying the tiny bottles
sold in the supermarket baking aisle.

Suzie's Holidaze Fudge

Susan Buetow
Du Quoin, IL

I've been making this fudge since I was 12 years old. I can remember the first year I made it for my Grandma. She loved it and took some to the beauty shop. All the gals there went nuts for it and wanted more. So began a little holiday moneymaker for a 12-year-old! I've never sold it as an adult, only as a kid living at home. I only make it at Christmastime, when I give it as gifts. This is a no-fail fudge and it is so yummy...it will melt in your mouth.

1/2 c. butter	12-oz. pkg. semi-sweet chocolate
1 c. milk	chips
4 c. sugar	2 sqs. unsweetened baking
2-1/2 c. mini marshmallows	chocolate
13-oz. pkg. milk chocolate candy	1 to 2 c. chopped nuts
bars, broken into pieces	

In a large saucepan over medium heat, melt butter with milk. Add sugar and mix well; stir in marshmallows. Continue to cook and stir until mixture comes to a rolling boil. Remove from heat. Add chocolates; mix well until melted. Fold in nuts. Pour onto a buttered 15"x10" jelly-roll pan. Quickly even out fudge with a spatula with a little butter on it. Set pan in refrigerator or on a cold porch until hardened; cut into small squares. Makes 4 dozen.

For a sweet greeting, pour fudge into small, shallow disposable baking pans. After fudge sets, pipe on a holiday greeting with colored icing. Wrap in clear cellophane and hand-deliver as edible Christmas cards...yum!

Gingerbread Men

LuLu Combs
Aberdeen, MD

These gingerbread men are a family favorite and a must for our Christmas gathering. I've always used this recipe that my grandmother shared with me. I can never seem to make enough! One year, I had gotten so behind on my baking, but I didn't dare show up without these little guys. So, I baked up a bunch, filled a squeeze bottle with the cookie glaze and let everyone decorate their own. They didn't seem to mind a bit and some of them preferred their gingerbread man naked...it was a win-win!

1/2 c. butter
1/2 c. sugar
1/2 c. molasses
1-1/2 t. white vinegar
1 egg, beaten
3 c. all-purpose flour

1/2 t. baking soda
1/4 t. salt
1/2 t. cinnamon
1/2 t. ground ginger
Optional: red cinnamon candies,
    raisins, candy sprinkles

In a saucepan over medium heat, melt butter with sugar, molasses and vinegar. Transfer to a bowl and let cool; add egg and set aside. In a separate bowl, whisk together flour, baking soda, salt and spices. Stir flour mixture into molasses mixture; mix well. Cover and refrigerate for one hour. Form 1/3 of dough into a ball; return remaining dough to the refrigerator. On a lightly floured surface, and adding a little flour to top of dough, roll out 1/8-inch thick. Dip cookie cutters into flour; cut out cookies and arrange on greased or parchment paper-lined baking sheets. Before baking, decorate with candies or raisins, if desired. Bake at 375 degrees for 8 to 12 minutes, just until edges are lightly golden. Cool on baking sheets for several minutes. Transfer to wire racks; cool completely. Repeat with remaining dough. Decorate with Cookie Glaze as desired. Makes 10 large or 14 small cookies.

Cookie Glaze:

2-1/4 c. powdered sugar
2 T. light corn syrup

1-1/2 to 2 T. milk

Whisk together powdered sugar, corn syrup and 1-1/2 tablespoons milk until smooth. If glaze is too stiff, add just a little more milk. Spoon into a squeeze bottle for decorating.

Holiday Desserts for Sharing

Grandma's Spritz Cookies

Signe Nelson
Portland, OR

I always knew Christmas was just around the corner when Mom baked these cookies. She got the recipe from her mother, who came here from Norway. We always had scrambled eggs the next morning to use up the leftover egg whites...good Norwegians don't let food go to waste!

1 lb. butter, room temperature
2 c. sugar
4 egg yolks
1 T. almond extract

2 T. whipping cream
5 c. all-purpose flour
Optional: candy sprinkles,
    colored sugar

In a large bowl, beat butter and sugar until mixed well. Add egg yolks, extract and cream; mix well. Gradually stir in flour. Cover and chill for about 20 minutes. Fill a cookie press with chilled dough; press out cookies onto ungreased baking sheets, 2 inches apart. Decorate cookies with sprinkles or colored sugar, if desired. Bake at 350 degrees for 8 to 10 minutes, until lightly golden around the edges but not browned. Makes 6 to 7 dozen.

Filled with cookies or candies, gift cards or movie passes,
a retro-style lunchbox makes a great gift box!

Giant Chocolate Chip Cookie

Penny Sherman
Ava, MO

This big cookie is so much fun to decorate, and it feeds a crowd. It's a great holiday party activity...just set out the cooled cookie in its pan alongside plenty of frosting colors and turn the kids loose!

1 c. plus 1 T. butter, divided	1 t. baking powder
1 c. light brown sugar, packed	1/2 t. salt
1 c. sugar	12-oz. pkg. semi-sweet
2 eggs, beaten	chocolate chips
1 t. vanilla extract	Garnish: favorite frosting,
2 c. all-purpose flour	candy sprinkles

In a large bowl, combine one cup butter and sugars. Beat with an electric mixer on medium speed until soft and fluffy. Add eggs, one at a time; beat until well blended. Stir in vanilla and set aside. In a separate bowl, stir together flour, baking powder and salt. Add flour mixture to butter mixture; beat until just blended. Fold in chocolate chips. Line a 15"x10" jelly-roll pan with parchment paper; lightly coat parchment paper and sides of pan with remaining butter. Spread batter evenly in pan. Bake at 350 degrees for 18 to 20 minutes, until lightly golden. Set pan on a wire rack; cool completely. Decorate cookie with frosting and sprinkles as desired. Cut into squares. Makes 2 dozen.

To stir up frosting in the reddest red, the greenest green and other extra bright holiday colors, choose paste-style food coloring...a little goes a long way!

Holiday Desserts for Sharing

Crustless Cranberry Pie

Judy Lange
Imperial, PA

Get all your friends together for coffee and a piece of pie after a morning of Christmas shopping. So yummy and easy!

3 c. fresh cranberries
1-1/2 c. sugar, divided
1/2 c. chopped walnuts
2 eggs

3/4 c. all-purpose flour
3/4 c. butter, melted
Garnish: whipped cream

Spread cranberries evenly in a 10" pie plate coated with non-stick vegetable spray. Sprinkle with 3/4 cup sugar and walnuts; stir into cranberries and set aside. In a large bowl, beat eggs until lemon-colored. Gradually stir in remaining sugar, flour and butter; beat until smooth. Spread mixture over cranberries and smooth with a spatula. Bake at 325 degrees for 45 minutes, or until bubbly and golden. Cut into wedges. Serve hot or cold, topped with whipped cream. Makes 8 servings.

For a scrumptious dessert in a jiffy, make an ice cream pie. Soften 2 pints of your favorite ice cream and spread in a crumb crust, then freeze. Garnish with whipped topping and cookie crumbs or fresh berries. Yummy!

Frozen Peppermint Dessert

Teresa Alley
Muncie, IN

*My grandmother loved her desserts! This is one she made
often at Christmastime. It's scrumptious.*

1 c. graham cracker crumbs,
  crushed
1 T. powdered sugar
2 T. butter, softened
8-oz. container frozen whipped
  topping, thawed

1/3 c. crushed peppermint
  candies
1-3/4 c. mini marshmallows
Optional: mini candy canes or
  round peppermint candies

In a bowl, combine crushed graham crackers, powdered sugar and
butter. Mix well and press into an ungreased 8"x8" baking pan; set
aside. Spoon whipped topping into a separate large bowl; fold in crushed
candies and marshmallows until well blended. Spoon over graham
cracker mixture and smooth out. Cover with aluminum foil; freeze for
3 hours or more. Before serving, allow to thaw slightly; cut into
squares. If desired, decorate each square with a mini candy cane or
a peppermint candy. Makes 9 servings.

Evergreen Punch

Sharon Tillman
Hampton, VA

Party perfect anytime!

48-oz. can pineapple juice
4 qts. cold water
4 0.13-oz. pkgs. unsweetened
  lemon-lime drink mix

2 to 3 c. sugar
2 qts. ginger ale, chilled
1 pt. lime sherbet

In a very large pitcher, combine pineapple juice, water and drink mix.
Add sugar to taste; stir well. Cover and chill. At serving time, pour
mixture into a punch bowl. Add ginger ale; stir gently. Float scoops of
sherbet on top and serve. Makes 7-1/2 quarts.

Holiday Desserts for Sharing

Crème de Menthe Pie

Breanne Rodgers
Duncansville, PA

We make this dessert every Christmas Eve. My boyfriend loves mint chocolate, and this pie has become his favorite. He really looks forward to it each year. We even now call it "Andy's Dessert."

24 chocolate sandwich cookies, crushed
1/4 c. butter, melted
2 8-oz. pkgs. cream cheese, softened
1-1/2 c. powdered sugar, divided
1/2 c. crème de menthe liqueur
2 c. whipping cream
Garnish: 1 sq. dark baking chocolate, shaved

Spray a 9" pie plate with non-stick vegetable spray; set aside. In a bowl, combine crushed cookies and butter; press into the bottom and sides of pie plate. In a separate bowl, combine cream cheese, 1/4 cup powdered sugar and crème de menthe. Stir until well blended and set aside. In a large bowl, combine cream and remaining powdered sugar. Beat with an electric mixer on high speed until stiff peaks form. Fold in cream cheese mixture; spoon into crust. Cover and chill for several hours. Garnish with shaved chocolate. Serves 6 to 8.

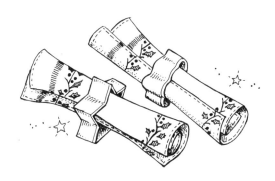

Use favorite cookie cutters for all kinds of holiday fun. Trace around them onto colorful paper for placecards and package tags...add glitter for sparkle. Cookie cutters can even trim a wreath or serve as napkin rings...clever!

Italian Christmas Cream

R. E. Rohlof
Hicksville, OH

*This creamy, fruit-filled dessert is perfect after a big holiday dinner.
If you don't have a Bundt pan, spoon the mixture into a bowl
and freeze, then scoop from the bowl for serving.*

2 firm bananas, peeled
   and sliced
2 c. seedless green grapes,
   halved
2 c. sour cream

1 c. maraschino cherries, drained
   and coarsely chopped
1 c. walnuts, coarsely chopped
1/2 c. sugar
1-1/2 t. lemon zest

Combine all ingredients in a large bowl; mix very well. Spoon into a
Bundt® pan coated with non-stick vegetable spray. Cover and freeze
for 8 hours or overnight. At serving time, let stand at room temperature
for 15 to 20 minutes. Turn out of pan onto a serving plate. Makes
8 servings.

Loosen a chilled dessert from the mold in a jiffy!
Dip the bottom of the mold in warm water. Set a plate
over the top of the mold and turn right-side up...
the dessert should slip out easily.

Holiday Desserts for Sharing

Almost Heaven Cake

Sandra Turner
Fayetteville, NC

This is an easy cake, but it tastes like you have put a lot of effort into making it! Once I took this to a church potluck, and one of the senior citizens in the congregation asked me if I would make this cake for his birthday later in the year. I was honored to do this for him.

18-1/2 oz. pkg. yellow cake mix
20-oz. can crushed pineapple
8-oz. pkg. cream cheese
2 c. milk
3.4-oz. pkg. instant French
    vanilla pudding mix
16-oz. container frozen whipped
    topping, thawed
7-oz. pkg. flaked coconut

Prepare cake according to package directions; bake in a greased 13"x9" baking pan. While cake is still hot, punch holes in the top with a fork. Spoon undrained pineapple over cake; let cool. In a large bowl, stir together cream cheese, milk and dry pudding mix until smooth; spoon over cake. Spread whipped topping over cake; sprinkle with coconut. Cover and refrigerate overnight before serving. Serves 12 to 15.

Candied cranberries are a lovely garnish. In a saucepan, bring one cup water and one cup sugar almost to a boil, stirring until sugar dissolves. Pour into a bowl and add one cup fresh cranberries; chill overnight. Drain cranberries well. Toss with superfine sugar to coat and dry on wax paper.

I'll Be Home for *Christmas* Cookbook

Christmas Plum Cake

Kathy Courington
Canton, GA

When my mother first made this, I asked her what it was, it was so good and rich! Easy too. A family favorite, great for the holidays.

2 c. sugar
1 c. oil
3 eggs
2 c. self-rising flour
1 t. cinnamon

Optional: 1 t. ground cloves
1 c. chopped nuts
2 4-oz. jars plum baby food
Garnish: powdered sugar

In a large bowl, beat together sugar, oil and eggs, beating after each egg; set aside. In another bowl, mix together flour, spices and nuts. Add flour mixture to sugar mixture; mix well and stir in baby food. Pour batter into a greased and floured Bundt® pan. Bake at 350 degrees for one hour, or until a toothpick inserted near the center tests clean. Cool cake in pan; turn out onto a plate. Sprinkle with powdered sugar. Serves 8 to 12.

Annie's Pound Cake

Karen Dean
New Market, MD

This cake is my favorite, so good and so easy to make. This was my great-grandmother's recipe, and I am the fourth generation to use it. It is so good with just about anything...fruit, syrup, ice cream or just a sprinkle of cinnamon.

1-1/2 c. butter, softened
16-oz. pkg. powdered sugar
6 eggs

1 T. vanilla extract
2-2/3 c. all-purpose flour

In a large bowl, blend together butter and powdered sugar. Stir in eggs, one at a time; mix in vanilla and flour. Pour batter into a greased and floured tube pan. Bake at 325 degrees for 1-1/2 hours, or until a toothpick inserted near the center tests clean. Cool; turn out onto a plate. Makes 20 servings.

For a holiday touch, serve coffee with eggnog
instead of cream.

Holiday Desserts for Sharing

Sandy's Pumpkin Spice Cake

Nichole Hawkins
Decatur, IN

This is one of the best recipes I've ever made. It's a moist and delicious cake for Thanksgiving and Christmas gatherings. I received this recipe from my Aunt Sandy, who was a home economics teacher for many years. Whenever I take this dessert somewhere, everyone asks for a copy of this recipe. It is so easy, and very budget-friendly for a great dessert!

18-1/4 oz. pkg. spice cake mix
15-oz. can pumpkin
8-oz. container frozen whipped
    topping, thawed

Garnish: cinnamon to taste

Prepare cake mix according to package directions. Add pumpkin to batter; mix thoroughly. Pour batter into a greased 13"x9" baking pan; bake according to directions on box. Cool cake completely in pan. Just before serving, spread with whipped topping; sprinkle with cinnamon. Serves 15 to 18.

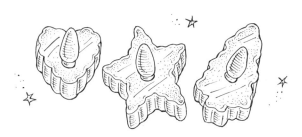

Whenever you shop for cookie cutters, candy sprinkles, flavoring extracts and other baking supplies, toss a few extras in the shopping cart. Wrap 'em up in a gift basket for a friend who loves to bake...she'll really appreciate your thoughtfulness!

I'll Be Home for *Christmas* Cookbook

Double Delicious Peanut Butter Cookies

Tamela James
Grove City, OH

This is one of my favorite recipes! I can remember my mom making these cookies when I was a little girl. I love the aroma they produce when baking, and the creamy peanut butter sandwiched between the warm cookies. I've made these for my own children too. I was even chosen the "Best Cook on the Block" by our hometown newspaper, and this is the recipe that was published with the article.

1-1/2 c. all-purpose flour
1/2 c. sugar
1/2 t. baking soda
1/4 t. salt
1/2 c. shortening

3/4 c. creamy peanut butter, divided
1/4 c. light corn syrup
1 t. milk

In a large bowl, sift together flour, sugar, baking soda and salt. Cut in shortening and 1/2 cup peanut butter until mixture resembles coarse meal. Blend in corn syrup and milk. Shape dough into a roll, 2 inches thick; wrap in plastic wrap and chill. Slice dough 1/8 to 1/4-inch thick. Place half of the dough slices on ungreased baking sheets; spread each with 1/2 teaspoon remaining peanut butter. Cover with remaining dough slices; seal edges with fork. Bake at 350 degrees for about 12 minutes. Cool slightly on baking sheets; remove to a wire rack and cool completely. Makes about 2 dozen.

After Christmas dinner, a simple dessert is perfect.
Serve assorted cookies accompanied by scoops of
pink peppermint ice cream.

Holiday Desserts for Sharing

Mom's Date-Nut Chews

Betty Kozlowski
Newnan, GA

Mom baked dozens & dozens of cookies every year at Christmastime to share with friends. These cookies were one of my favorites.

2/3 c. all-purpose flour
3/4 t. baking powder
1/2 t. salt
1 c. brown sugar, packed
1 c. chopped dates

1 c. chopped nuts
2 eggs
1 t. vanilla extract
Garnish: powdered sugar

In a large bowl, sift together flour, baking powder, salt and brown sugar. Stir in dates and nuts. Beat eggs and vanilla in a small bowl; blend into flour mixture. Pour batter into a greased 8"x8" baking pan. Bake at 350 degrees for 35 minutes. While still warm, cut into one-inch squares; roll into balls. Roll in powdered sugar, coating well. Makes 4 dozen.

Mudballs

Anne Ptacnik
Yuma, CO

My Grandpa & Grandma Korf liked to make plates of candies and cookies to take to neighbors and friends at Christmastime. This special treat was always included, and I think of them every time I make this yummy chocolate & peanut butter candy. You might know them as buckeye candy!

1/2 c. butter, melted
2 c. powdered sugar
2 c. crunchy peanut butter

3-1/2 c. crispy rice cereal
12-oz. pkg. milk chocolate chips
2 T. paraffin wax, chopped

In a large bowl, mix together butter, powdered sugar, peanut butter and cereal. Form into one-inch balls; set aside. In a saucepan over low heat, melt chocolate chips with paraffin wax. Dip balls into chocolate with a fork; place on wax paper to set. Makes 3 dozen.

Make a gift of homemade candy even sweeter...
place individual candies in mini paper muffin cups
and arrange in a decorated box.

Kolatchi

Karen Wilson
Defiance, OH

*My mom got this recipe from a Hungarian co-worker more than
50 years ago and it's still one of our favorite Christmas cookies.
Raspberry or apricot preserves can be substituted for the nut filling.*

1 env. active dry yeast
1 c. sour cream
4 c. all-purpose flour
4 egg yolks, room temperature

1 whole egg, room temperature
1 lb. butter, room temperature
1/8 t. salt
Garnish: sugar

In a small bowl, dissolve yeast in sour cream; set aside. In a large
bowl, combine flour, egg yolks, egg, butter and salt. Stir in yeast
mixture until thoroughly combined. Dough will be stiff. Cover and
refrigerate overnight. Divide dough into 4 balls. On a floured surface,
roll out one ball at a time, 1/8 to 1/4-inch thick. Cut into 1-1/2 inch
squares. Place a teaspoon of Nut Filling in the center of each square.
Fold over 2 opposite corners to overlap in the center and press to seal;
coat in sugar. Place on parchment paper-lined baking sheets. Bake at
375 degrees for 12 minutes. Makes 10 dozen.

Nut Filling:

1 lb. ground walnuts or pecans
1/2 c. sugar

2 egg whites, room temperature
1 t. vanilla extract

Combine all ingredients; mix well.

Découpage Grandma's favorite cookie recipe onto the lid
of a tin and fill with cookies...sure to be appreciated!

Holiday Desserts for Sharing

Taylor-Made Toffee Treats

Judy Taylor
Butler, MO

A family recipe given to me by an aunt many years ago.
It's so delicious and easy to make.

1 c. butter
1 c. brown sugar, packed
1 egg yolk
1 c. all-purpose flour

6 1.55-oz. milk chocolate candy
  bars, broken
1 c. chopped pecans

In a large bowl, blend butter, brown sugar and egg yolk. Add flour; mix well. Spread batter in a greased 15"x10" jelly-roll pan. Bake at 350 degrees for 10 to15 minutes, until dough appears set in the center. Immediately top with candy bars and let stand until melted; spread chocolate. Top with pecans. Let stand until set; cut into squares. Makes 3 dozen.

Homemade Hot Chocolate Mix

Karen Gentry
Eubank, KY

My mother and daughter used to drink this all the time and they loved it. It makes amazing Christmas presents...just fill gift baskets with a jar of mix, a bag of mini marshmallows and a mug.

25.6-oz pkg. powdered milk
16-oz. pkg. chocolate drink mix

7-oz. jar non-dairy creamer
1/2 c. powdered sugar

Mix together all ingredients in a large airtight container. Cover and store. Directions: Add 1/2 cup of mix to 3/4 cup boiling water; stir well. Makes 18 to 20 servings.

Cranberry Pudding with Hot Butter Sauce

Nancy Lambert
West Jordan, UT

We make this every Christmas Eve! It is so rich and delicious. This recipe can be doubled and baked in a 13x9 pan. I also like to make it in muffin tins for individual cakes.

1 T. butter	1/2 t. salt
1 c. sugar	1 c. evaporated milk
2 c. all-purpose flour	2 c. fresh cranberries
2 t. baking powder	

In a large bowl, blend together butter and sugar; set aside. In another bowl, sift together flour, baking powder and salt. Add flour mixture to butter mixture alternately with milk, beating after each addition. Fold in cranberries. Pour batter into a greased 8"x8" baking pan. Bake at 350 degrees for 25 to 30 minutes. Serve slices of pudding topped with Hot Butter Sauce. Serves 8.

Hot Butter Sauce:

1/2 c. butter	1/2 c. whipping cream
3/4 c. sugar	1 t. vanilla extract

In a small saucepan over medium heat, combine all ingredients except vanilla. Bring to a boil; reduce heat to low and simmer for 10 minutes. Remove from heat; stir in vanilla.

The holiday season is a good time to check your spice rack for freshness. Crush a pinch of each spice... if it has a fresh, zingy scent, it's still good.

Holiday Desserts for **Sharing**

Vermont Maple Pumpkin Pie

Shirley Howie
Foxboro, MA

My mom always made this pie at Thanksgiving and Christmas, using our very own maple syrup that we made on our small farm in Vermont. When I make it now, it always brings back those warm, wonderful memories of holidays spent with loved ones.

15-oz. can pumpkin
1 c. brown sugar, packed
2 eggs, beaten
2 T. all-purpose flour
1 t. cinnamon
1/2 t. ground ginger
1/4 t. ground cloves

1/2 t. nutmeg
1/2 t. salt
12-oz. can evaporated milk
1/2 c. pure maple syrup
10-inch pie crust, unbaked
Garnish: whipped cream

In a large bowl, mix together pumpkin, brown sugar, eggs, flour, spices and salt until smooth and well combined. Gradually stir in evaporated milk and maple syrup until fully blended. Pour into unbaked pie crust. Bake at 350 degrees for 60 to 65 minutes, until a knife tip inserted in the center comes out clean. Cool completely before serving. Garnish slices with a dollop of whipped cream. Makes 8 servings.

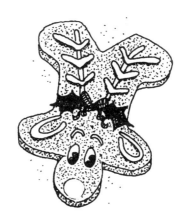

Reindeer cookies! Flip a gingerbread man cookie upside-down. Pipe on antlers, ears and a face, and add a bright red gumdrop nose. Simple!

213

Grandma Cora's Russian Tea Cakes

Leona Krivda
Belle Vernon, PA

When my grandma made these cookies, I loved to eat them warm, even thought she always chased me away from them. The things you remember! These are usually on my Christmas baking list, and now my family gets to enjoy them too.

1 c. butter
1/2 c. powdered sugar
1 t. vanilla extract
2-1/4 c. all-purpose flour

1/4 t. salt
3/4 c. nuts, finely chopped
Garnish: additional powdered
   sugar

In a large bowl, combine butter, powdered sugar and vanilla; blend well. Add flour and salt; mix very well. Stir in nuts. Cover and chill for about one hour. Roll dough into one-inch balls; place on ungreased baking sheets. Cookies will not spread while baking. Bake at 400 degrees for 10 to 12 minutes. Roll warm cookies in powdered sugar. Cool; roll again in powdered sugar. Makes 2 dozen.

Rolling dough into cookie-size balls is child's play... perfect for kids learning to bake. Make a sample dough ball so they'll know what size to make, set out baking sheets and let the kids take over!

Holiday Desserts for Sharing

Mint Chip Cake Mix Cookies

Rachel Phillips
New Castle, DE

I love to bake this simple four-ingredient cookie recipe and enjoy the flavors of Christmas with a cup of hot cocoa, or share with a neighbor or shut-in. For a change of pace, use peanut butter chips instead of the mint chips.

18-1/2 oz. pkg. chocolate
   cake mix
2 eggs, beaten

1/3 c. oil
10-oz. pkg. dark chocolate &
   mint chips

In a large bowl, beat together dry cake mix, eggs and oil. Stir in chocolate chips. Roll dough into one-inch balls. Place on lightly greased baking sheets; flatten slightly with the bottom of a cup dipped in sugar. Bake at 350 degrees for 10 minutes, or until a slight indentation remains when lightly touched. Cool on pans for one minute. Transfer to wire racks; cool. Makes 2 dozen.

Santa's Happy Holiday Cookies

Lisa Staib
Ash Flat, AR

These are just the happiest, reddest, tastiest cookies. Right out of the bowl they're adorable and yummy. Nibble, decorate, share, save some for Santa...and enjoy! Ho-ho-ho!

15-oz. pkg. red velvet cake mix
2 eggs, beaten
1/2 c. oil

1-1/4 c. white chocolate chips
Optional: candy sprinkles

In a large bowl, beat together dry cake mix, eggs and oil until smooth. Stir in chocolate chips. Cover and chill for 45 minutes. Form dough into one-inch balls. Place on greased baking sheets; add sprinkles, if desired. Bake at 350 degrees for 10 to 13 minutes. Cool on pans for 5 minutes. Transfer to wire racks; cool. Makes 2 dozen.

Chocolate Chip Snowballs

M'lissa Johnson
Baytown, TX

It just isn't Christmas to us without snowball cookies, and what could possibly make them better? Chocolate chips! My kids love to help with rolling these yummies into balls and then rolling them in powdered sugar.

1 c. butter, room temperature
1/2 c. powdered sugar
1 t. vanilla extract
2 1/4 c. all-purpose flour
1/2 t. salt

1 c. regular or mini semi-sweet
   chocolate chips
Garnish: additional powdered
   sugar

In a large bowl, combine butter, powdered sugar and vanilla. Beat with an electric mixer on medium speed until light and fluffy. Add flour and salt; beat until well blended. Stir in chocolate chips. Cover and chill dough at least one hour. Roll into balls by tablespoonfuls; place on greased baking sheets. Bake at 375 degrees for 7 to 10 minutes, until lightly golden on the bottom. Cool cookies for 2 to 3 minutes, until cool enough to handle. Roll cookies in powdered sugar until well coated. Place on a wire rack; cool completely. If desired, roll cookies again in powdered sugar. Makes 4 dozen.

Need a sleighful of gifts for co-workers? Pick up vintage coffee mugs at thrift shops for a song. Fill them with cookies and wrap in festive cellophane...sure to be a hit!

Holiday Desserts for Sharing

Dirty Snowballs

Michelle Caldwell
Totz, KY

These treats are fun to share! If you want your "dirty snowballs" even dirtier, add some crushed dark chocolate sandwich cookies. You may need to add a little more candy coating.

1 c. "snow" (shredded coconut)
1 c. "sticks" (broken pretzel thins)
1 c. "pebbles" (chopped pecans)
1 c. "grit" (crispy rice cereal)
12-oz. pkg. "melted snow" (melted white candy coating)

In a large bowl, combine all ingredients except candy coating; toss to mix and set aside. In a microwave-soft bowl, microwave candy coating in 30-second intervals, stirring after each, until melted and completely smooth. Pour melted candy coating over ingredients in bowl; stir to coat thoroughly. Working quickly before mixture sets up, press firmly into a small scoop to shape; place on parchment or wax paper to set. Makes 2-1/2 dozen.

Family fun...build a yummy gingerbread house together
and top it off with chocolate bar doors and shutters!

INDEX

INDEX

INDEX

Find Gooseberry Patch
wherever you are!

www.gooseberrypatch.com

Call us toll-free at 1·800·854·6673

handknit mittens · strings of popcorn

homemade candy

sugar cookies

letters to Santa

holly & mistletoe

paper snowflakes · curling ribbons

U.S. to Metric Recipe Equivalents

Volume Measurements

1/4 teaspoon	1 mL
1/2 teaspoon	2 mL
1 teaspoon	5 mL
1 tablespoon = 3 teaspoons	15 mL
2 tablespoons = 1 fluid ounce	30 mL
1/4 cup	60 mL
1/3 cup	75 mL
1/2 cup = 4 fluid ounces	125 mL
1 cup = 8 fluid ounces	250 mL
2 cups = 1 pint =16 fluid ounces	500 mL
4 cups = 1 quart	1 L

Weights

1 ounce	30 g
4 ounces	120 g
8 ounces	225 g
16 ounces = 1 pound	450 g

Oven Temperatures

300° F	150° C
325° F	160° C
350° F	180° C
375° F	190° C
400° F	200° C
450° F	230° C

Baking Pan Sizes

Square

8x8x2 inches	2 L = 20x20x5 cm
9x9x2 inches	2.5 L = 23x23x5 cm

Rectangular

13x9x2 inches	3.5 L = 33x23x5 cm

Loaf

9x5x3 inches	2 L = 23x13x7 cm

Round

8x1-1/2 inches	1.2 L = 20x4 cm
9x1-1/2 inches	1.5 L = 23x4 cm